STRAIGHT / WHITE / MALE

Edited by
GLENN R. BUCHER

FORTRESS PRESS   Philadelphia

COPYRIGHT © 1976 BY FORTRESS PRESS

Library of Congress Catalog Card Number 75–13039

ISBN 0–8006–1209–4

4974J75   Printed in U.S.A.   1–1209

ᴐ the women and men who lived in
Westminster House on The College
of Wooster campus during the years
1971–74, this book is dedicated.
We know the joys and sorrows of life
together; of entrenched slaveries to
the old; of reluctant openness to
the new.   May we continue to covet
liberation as a way of life, and
new human alternatives as the means
for living out freedom in the world.

Contents

Preface vii

Part One: Attention! Honkies, Sexists, and Straights

1. The Enemy: He Is Us 2
   Glenn R. Bucher
2. Confessions 11
   Glenn R. Bucher

Part Two: From the Slaves: To the Masters

3. Black Power and Straight White Males 30
   Benjamin D. Berry
4. Feminism and Straight White Males 40
   Patricia R. Hill
5. Gay Liberation and Straight White Males 51
   Charles R. Gaver

Part Three: From the Masters: To Themselves

6. The Oppressor Dehumanized 72
   Glenn R. Bucher
7. The Meaning of Whiteness 85
   Patricia N. Dutcher
8. Maleness and Heterosexuality 99
   Charles E. Lindner

Part Four: Toward Whiteness, Maleness, and Sexuality
           in a New Perspective: A Dialogue

9. Liberation for Straight White Males 114
   Glenn R. Bucher and Charles E. Lindner
10. An Agenda 134
    Glenn R. Bucher and Charles E. Lindner

Contributors 149

Preface

Straight/White/Male is not an ordinary book. It requires receptivity to an unusual format, openness to the flux of a theme developing, and a personal commitment—that you, the reader, appropriate existentially what is said.

The table of contents reveals our distinctive format. The work has one editor and five contributors but is not a traditional symposium; it concludes with two chapters of dialogue. This arrangement is intentional. It accentuates the *corporateness* of human liberation, which is neither an isolated experience nor an individualistic enterprise but a collective process including, ultimately, all human beings who struggle to overcome depersonalizing forces. Separation is necessary as persons affirm unique identities in the pursuit of freedom. But as liberation cuts through *social* dehumanizations, it necessarily involves other persons. The book has taken on a format consistent with the message it intends to convey.

The completeness associated with most published works is missing here because human liberation is a process, not an event. The material captures, at a moment, the dynamics of flight from slavery to freedom. Our words are tentative. We can speak of liberation only as it continues to happen.

Finally, this work is undisguisedly personal. It is defined by praxis, the combining of thought and action. If to be academic is to be dispassionate, this book is an intellectual failure, because the context for our praxis is existential struggle. Freedom has encountered us. Our own enslavements have been addressed. So, hopefully, will it be with every reader.

The book was conceived and compiled by Glenn R. Bucher. A husband, father, and professor, he was socialized as a typical straight white male in America. Thanks to those not similarly produced—blacks, women, and homosexuals—Bucher eventually discovered that to enjoy the status he did, and to participate in the social roles he had, was to rub shoulders with the sexism,

the paternalism, and the authoritarianism indigenous to those social categories. To believe that he was also a *person* entitled to
the quest for wholeness was to begin to confront these dehumanizing realities. It was to risk liberation. That is happening. Out of that risk the idea for this book emerged. Hence,
Bucher is responsible for Part One, thoughts on the dehumanized
oppressor, and—with a colleague—two chapters on what straight
white males can do about their own liberation. As compiler of
this document, he is also responsible for the organizational structure as it developed in the editorial process.

The contemporary freedom struggles of blacks, women, and
homosexuals are producing self-awareness among those groups,
and indictments of straight white males implicated in their oppression. This is beginning to stir up reluctant straight white
male consciousness. *Straight/White/Male* is about the possibilities for liberation emerging from that consciousness-raising.
But before those possibilities could be entertained, it was necessary to hear about liberation movements among the oppressed,
and their implications for the oppressor. In Part Two Benjamin
D. Berry, Patricia R. Hill, and Charles R. Gaver write of black
power, feminism, and gay liberation from the inside. What is
significant not only about their written contributions but also
about themselves is this: they combine strong commitments to
quests for identity with a redemptive openness to straight white
males who need liberation as well.

Parts One and Two thus define the straight white male problem;
the slaves have spoken to the masters. Parts Three and Four
point toward solutions; the masters can also speak to themselves.

What the masters shall initially learn about the straight white
male predicament is presented in Part Three. Following the
Bucher discussion of how the oppressor is dehumanized, Patricia
N. Dutcher, a white woman, and Charles E. Lindner, a straight
white male, direct attention to the facts, dilemmas, and hopes
attached to whiteness, maleness, and heterosexual preference.
Dutcher's whiteness and femininity place her in a unique position
vis-à-vis liberation: she is from the black perspective a victor, but
as a woman also a victim. She lives with this ambiguity and is
committed to sorting through it. By viewing all liberation struggles in the context of the larger economic realities of a white-
dominated international order she adds to the discussion dimensions too often obscured.

Charles E. Linder speaks, then, about maleness and heterosexual preference. He is a male critical of maleness, having known in himself and witnessed in an upper-middle-class suburban community what the American social structure has done to straight white males and what they have done to *it*. He seeks personal and social alternatives as he works at who he is and wants to become.

But it is not enough to be analytical and critical. Hence the discussion moves on quickly to a constructive dialogue about liberation for straight white males. Part Four, positive and hopeful, can only be viewed within the framework provided by Parts One through Three. But it goes beyond them as the two most-traditionally straight white male contributors, Bucher and Lindner, talk together about emergent liberation for those brought to an awareness of themselves by the mid-to-late twentieth century quests for freedom. The dialogue moves from theory to praxis: from talk of what liberation is to contending with how it can be operationalized in an agenda.

The corporateness reflected in this book was not instantaneously achieved. Nor was it called forth merely by the project. To Robert A. Martin, Kenneth E. Plusquellec, Mary K. Bucher, and Glenn R. Bucher belongs the credit for having initiated a living situation which brought together, among others, four of the contributors to this book. It was in Westminster House, a cooperative coeducational living unit on the campus of The College of Wooster (Wooster, Ohio) where a faculty family and three groups of young adults began to encounter themselves, each other, and the tasks of liberation, that *Straight/White/Male* had its inception. There, the corporateness which is evident here found its reason for being.

Some may conclude from this Preface that *Straight/White/Male* is full of hate, guilt, and despair. To the extent that we despise the unreconstructed whiteness, maleness, and sexuality apparent in American society today, there is hate. Any straight white male who knows what he has done to "Others" must be aware of guilt. Despair may be the result. In fact, any straight white male who is not somewhat distraught over his own condition—and that of blacks, women, and homosexuals as a consequence of his own—needs to engage in serious self-examination. But *Straight/White/Male* is a symbol of hope, fundamentally; otherwise we would not have written it. In the whiteness, maleness, and sexuality underlying that which causes so much despair, there are some sources of strength, prospects for change, and marks of resurrection.   Human liberation *can* begin to *happen* among straight white males—that is at the heart of this work, and its main thesis.   With realistic despair, yet with excited hope, the reader is invited to join the quest.

In the preparation of this work, the editor indebted himself to many in addition to the five contributors.   Beyond her thoughtful chapter, Patricia R. Hill's editorial assistance was invaluable; not only did she urge the inclusion of a discussion on homosexuality, but she also provided helpful comments at every stage of development.   Without the typing skills of Deborah Cornelius and Joanne Yoder, the manuscript would not have received the time and care evident here.   Finally, Mary K. Bucher, Christina H. Bucher, and Timothy J. Bucher inspired and tolerated the work this book demanded; without their support it would not be.

G.R.B.

Part One

Attention! Honkies, Sexists, and Straights

Over the past ten years, the cultural hegemony dominating
America has begun to erode as different segments of the population have come to see that America has been exclusively defined according to the needs and desires of a ruling elite of
white, middle-aged, male heterosexuals. In turn blacks, the
young, women, and homosexuals have challenged this
hegemony and as a result America is more fragmented, more
divided, and yet freer than ever before in its history.*

—DENNIS ALTMAN

1. The Enemy: He Is Us

Glenn R. Bucher

There is a new language alive in America today. Its vibrancy and
power stand out against the dull, confused, everyday chatter of
our society. Though of recent birth, this language has roots that
go deeper than the contemporary scene. It is as old as the He-
brew patriarch's demand: "Let my people go!" The new language reflects the vitality of its heritage: it has already become a
powerful form of communication among certain Americans.
Like all language, it is a product of community, and descriptive of
the world in which those who use it live. But it is more than that!
It is also an *interpretation* of that world, of America's place in it,
and of the communities of alienation from which the language
arises. Human beings respond to the messages and challenges of
their experience through the languages they create and use. So it
is with this new language—the language of human liberation.

Word symbols are the essence of every language. The language of human liberation is no exception. Its symbols have
been conceived in particular communities and have emerged to
enter contemporary vocabulary. The most explosive and affront-

ing words, not surprisingly, have become the most popular: honkie and white racist, masculinist pig and male chauvinist, and straight and sexist. There are groups for whom this language is indigenous: Black Panthers and Black Nationalists, National Organization for Women and Society for Cutting Up Men, and Gay Activist Alliance and Gay Liberation Front. The writings of specific authors have become part of this language, too: *If They Come In the Morning* by Angela Davis and *To Die for the People* by Huey Newton, *The Second Sex* by Simone de Beauvoir and *Sexual Politics* by Kate Millet, and *Homosexual: Oppression and Liberation* by Dennis Altman and *Lesbian Nation* by Jill Johnston.[1]

The new language is not only descriptive, but also active. Oppression, exploitation, and alienation depict what has happened to the victimized, whereas liberation, freedom, and humanization announce what must occur. All are linguistic tools which indicate the human conditions against and toward which the language of human liberation is directed.

From communities of alienated blacks, women, and homosexuals who struggle toward self-affirmation amidst oppressive internal and external social psychological forces the new language has arisen. The world in which these alienated communities exist includes contemporary America and the "unyoung, uncolored, and unpoor" syndrome of international society.[2] The time, though not devoid of history, is now. The goal of the "movements" is personal and social liberation for those who are oppressed. The oppressor is the straight white male. This book is about the oppressor. We have met him, and he is US!

The search for individual and corporate selfhood among blacks, women, and gays is neither new nor uniquely American. Neither is the quest confined to those three groups. "The gay movement," "women's lib," "civil rights"—in substance date back at least to the country's settlement. Even then, the dominance of whiteness, maleness, and heterosexuality required that those who were non-white or non-male or non-heterosexual struggle for psychological and social survival. Nor are such efforts the exclusive property of America's alienated. The present revolts of the colonized against the colonizers in the Third World make that clear.[3] *Straight/White/Male,* however, is primarily a contemporary statement, conceived and born amidst the frustration and despair, the excitement and hope, of liberation American-style.

The appearance of this document will please some, especially

certain straight white males. It may be viewed as a long-overdue
defense of the unjustly abused straight white male, presently
suffering—though not much, actually—at the hands of those who
shout Honkie! Chauvinist! and Straight! The book will be *inac-
curately* perceived by them as a legitimate defense of the authority, the ingenuity—perhaps even the superiority—of the straight
white male. After all, those who built the American monument
to technocracy deserve more respect than is presently accorded
by coons, chicks, and faggots!

Blacks, women, and gays are likely to smile cynically upon
seeing this statement. The straight white male is so much the
oppressor, it will be argued, that any response to charges can only
be illegitimately defensive. Straight white males, so it will be
claimed, have no other role in contemporary liberation struggles
than that of hopeful, passive observer. Perhaps they will be
freed from their unliberated condition as masters when the
slaves—blacks, women, and gays—free themselves.

Another group may have still a third response. Maintaining a
middle course between reactionary anticipation and disbelieving
disgust, liberal straight white males will insist, erroneously, that
this book constitutes a mild slapping of the hairy, masculine hand.
It will be viewed as partial recognition that straight white male
behavior necessitates adjustments in order to take account of
injustices perpetrated upon discriminated-against Americans.

If blacks, women, and gays are not interested in *Straight/
White/Male,* if traditional straight white males fail to find the de-
fenses so desperately needed, and if liberal straight white males
are confronted by radical charges and demands that they are not
prepared to entertain, then who is left? Readers approaching the
book from any of these three perspectives will be sorely disap-
pointed. The document is not a reaction, but a response. It is
not a defense, but an inquiry. It is not a bland confession, but a
tart thinking through. It is an effort to examine the predicament
of straight white males in American society as that which has
been recently exposed and to consider ways in which straight
white males can begin to entertain their own thoughts of
liberation—not that straight white males are oppressed, but they
do need to be liberated from dehumanization.

THE PRESENT AS PARADOX

To speak of straight white male liberation as a response to the
liberation pursuits of blacks, women, and gays is to encounter a

paradox of no mean proportions. Those who write of liberation have defined this paradox more accurately than any of the popular responses. The relationship between black liberation and the liberation of whites is described by James H. Cone in *Liberation: A Black Theology of Liberation:*

> When the oppressed affirm their freedom by refusing to behave according to the master's rules, they not only liberate themselves from oppression, but they also liberate the oppressors from an enslavement to their illusions. Therefore, the basic error of white comments about their own oppression is the assumption that they know the nature of their enslavement.[4]

Likewise, male liberation within the crucible of the women's struggle is anticipated by Betty Roszak in this manner:

> Women's liberation will thus inevitably bring with it, as a concomitant, men's liberation. Men, no less than women, are imprisoned by the heavy carapace of their sexual stereotype. The fact that they gain more advantages and privileges from women's oppression has blinded them to their own bondage.[5]

Dennis Altman puts it most succinctly: "Gay liberation liberates straights as much as gays."[6]

The life stories of James Cone, Betty Roszak, and Dennis Altman overlap at points. From the standpoint of dominance in America, all are *social marginales*—a black male, a white woman, and a male homosexual. All see themselves as objects of social exploitation, as oppressed members of American society. Cone, Roszak, and Altman are active participants in the respective struggles for liberation that presently characterize the mood and activity of some blacks, women, and gays. Finally, all share a common view of who it is that has perpetrated the oppression of which they are the victims—straight white males! Here is the paradox: Cone, Roszak, and Altman suggest: (1) that straight white males are as enslaved as blacks, women, and gays, and (2) that straight white males can do nothing about their freedom except wait—wait for straight white male liberation as the *by-product* of freedom secured by others.

So far as possible, this paradox must be acknowledged. In obvious and obscure ways, the masters in the society are more dehumanized than the slaves. The former have learned to be most psychologically dependent upon their status. There is little talk of straight white male liberation amidst the current criticisms of and challenges to them. That is proof of dehumanization. Masters are not prepared to understand their own imprisonment;

when confronted, their responses include ignoring it and discounting it.

Is it so, then, that straight white males have only the option left by Cone, Roszak, and Altman—to wait and expect freedom as a by-product of the struggles of others? If so, this book is a contradiction; if their liberation is a by-product, then straight white males have no business talking about it. Perhaps the only option is to wait! To this suggestion, however, both a yes and a no are in order.

Yes, because as blacks, women, and gays move from what has been made of them to an authentic, self-determined affirmation of who they are and want to become, the objects of straight white male oppression will begin to disappear, leaving them with defaulted freedom. If there are no slaves, there can be no masters!

No, because straight white males cannot afford to wait that long and that passively for freedom. As an indirect result of oppressing blacks, women, and gays, males have dehumanized themselves. We have become the social products of our own productivity. We have succumbed to roles and behavior that have transformed us into special persons. Admittedly, we enjoy the status, however unconsciously acquired. Though that questionable privilege will be most eloquently exposed and undermined by the liberation of those we have oppressed, there is no reason why we cannot tentatively examine it, and do something about it, ourselves.

There is a practical reason why straight white males must begin to understand themselves independently of, though in conjunction with, blacks, women, and gays. Our social privilege is on the wane. If you don't believe that, look at almost any advertisement of a job vacancy these days. In the academic marketplace it would include this statement: "Women and minority group candidates are encouraged to apply."[7] Before our liberation is handed to us, we will find ourselves the least desirable candidates for job vacancies. That is important, because we have defined ourselves by what we do—the second question asked of strangers at any cocktail party. We are headed for a crisis of substantial proportion. We will be forced to consider our own self-identities long before we are liberated from them.

The Future as Struggle

Why, then, has an inquiry about the liberation of straight white males now seen the light of day? Because these persons are in trouble! We have been presented with a host of difficult questions which we cannot ignore. We have been shocked and shaken. There have been external jolts to our being, and our unpreparedness to consider them exceeds even our unwillingness to do so. But the questions and the inquisitors will not go away until, on the other side of a legion of liberation struggles that have only begun, human beings can begin to define in new ways who they are and want to be, unencumbered by the stereotypes of old.

Because certain questions have molded the purposes of this book they must be aired: What does it mean to be a straight white male in contemporary American society? What are the liberation movements of blacks, women, and homosexuals saying to and revealing about the straight white male? To what extent and in what ways are straight white males themselves dehumanized? What does it mean to speak of whiteness and maleness and heterosexuality? What are the resources available with which to begin the struggle for straight white male liberation? What is a liberated straight white male? There are other questions. None seem more basic than these. Whether he knows it or not, every straight white male has been summoned by time and circumstance to answer, and answer we must. Though we can learn much about ourselves from blacks, women, and gays, the times require that we also speak to, with, and for ourselves. We shall do just that, but not in such a fashion as to render the discourse unintelligible to others.

To concern myself with straight white male liberation is not to undertake an objective, impassionate, and analytical study. That is impossible for one who has been traditionally white and male and straight. Objectivity, reason, and analysis are not out of order, but they will be combined with the subjectivity, passion, and confession born of being what I am. *Straight/White/Male* is the product of existential struggle. Its roots go back to the late 1960s and a black metropolitan multiversity where, as a member of the white faculty minority, I discovered what black persons in America have known since they were brought here as slaves: the psychological anguish of living in a world where one's being derives no support from the nature of the world in which he or she lives. As Martin Luther King, Jr. said about his black experience in a white world, so it was with white involvement in a black world: one is judged by the color of one's skin, not by the content of one's character. "Of course," some will say, "blacks can be racist, too!" But this was not the conclusion I drew from my experience. What I learned rather, was that white people in America have no idea what it means to be a *social marginale* in a culture whose language, customs, behaviorisms, and attitudes are imperialistically dominated by the majority—nor any wisdom regarding how they personally participate daily in those dominations.

The fires of torment to this white soul, derived from a short life in the black world, will be discussed in chapter 2; suffice it to say that once one views whiteness within the artificially-dominant context of blackness, there is no returning to the uninformed innocence of previous times. One has a single choice: to ignore the existential anguish *or* to seek out a fuller comprehension of whiteness in American society and in the world, an understanding that takes seriously the white racial burden dating back to 1619 when black slaves were first brought to this land by white people. To choose the latter option is to begin the trek up the long road of white liberation.

The notion of maleness, for me, is of more recent awareness and experience. This should not have been. Why was it not obvious that whiteness cannot be separated from maleness? That their connection was obscured speaks eloquently of the dimensions of the male problem. Again, it was outside forces that motivated me to seek understanding. When one is surrounded by a five-year-old daughter and a one-year-old biracial son whose lives emerge through a complex of freedom and acculturation; by a partner whose own struggles for authentic womanhood affect those with whom she relates; and by college students who, though sometimes not sure whether they are prepared to do what they say, have commitments to a liberated personhood within the crucibles of masculinity and femininity—and to "a new heaven and earth" to go with it—then not to begin to contemplate maleness is not to be alive. It is to be indeed dead!

The matter of heterosexuality followed closely behind an emerging awareness of masculinity vis-à-vis freedom for women. Contemporaries who have remained open to expressions of love irrespective of the sex from which they arise have forced this contributor to see heterosexuality as a significant though not exclusive form of relationship. It is apparent that traditional definitions of masculinity, as they pertain to females and males, are narrow and inhuman. Social norms have been permitted to define sexuality in unhealthy ways. Combine this with what these same norms have done to lesbians and homosexuals, and one comes to see how necessary a discussion of sexuality is to a contemporary statement on straight white male liberation.

Finally, it is the cultural situation of the present moment that has brought to a head the need to speak of liberation, white and male and straight. The struggles for social justice of a previous decade are over, but the impetus for personal and social liberation born in that time is, in a new and different way, alive. With the virtual demise of those earlier movements went the social awareness which American society needs so desperately today. But with them also went a liberalism which, though well-meaning, was shallow in nature, a liberalism which permitted people to think, to speak, and to act on behalf of social justice without considering their own personal participation in the injustices they decried. Old liberal commitments failed to cut deeply enough to affect the lifestyles of the committed. The failure of social movements built upon this liberalism is unfortunate, though not surprising. Because its roots of belief and conviction did not penetrate to the heart of each individual and of the society, the movements succumbed. They were not radical enough!

Hence, we find ourselves in a new situation in America, with two options: a return to pre-movement days, to the unexamined American life and the personal and social innocence of the post-World War Two period; or a leap forward toward a new tomorrow where the fires of truth, honesty, and deep commitment will forge out of the chaos of today, a new life for new people in a new world. *Straight/White/Male* is born out of necessity for the latter choice!

NOTES

*Dennis Altman, *Homosexual: Oppression and Liberation* (New York: Outerbridge & Lazard, 1971), p. 47.

1. Angela Davis, *If They Come in the Morning* (Chicago: Third World Press, 1973); Huey Newton, *To Die for the People* (New York: Random House, 1972); Simone de Beauvoir, *The Second Sex* (New York: Bantam Books, 1953); Kate Millet, *Sexual Politics* (New York: Doubleday & Co., 1970); Dennis Altman, *Homosexual: Oppression and Liberation* (New York: Outerbridge & Lazard, 1971); and Jill Johnston, *Lesbian Nation* (New York: Simon & Schuster, 1973).

2. Colin Morris, *Unyoung, Uncolored, Unpoor* (Nashville: Abingdon Press, 1969).

3. Albert Memmi, *The Colonizer and the Colonized* (New York: Viking Press, 1965).

4. James H. Cone, *Liberation: A Black Theology of Liberation* (Philadelphia: Lippincott, 1970), pp. 185–86.

5. Betty Roszak, "The Human Continuum," in *Masculine/Feminine,* ed. Betty Roszak and Theodore Roszak (New York: Harper & Row, 1969), pp. 303–4.

6. Altman, *Homosexual: Oppression and Liberation,* p. 233.

7. "Bulletin Board," *The Chronicle of Higher Education,* 7, no. 29 (April 23, 1973):14.

History made the WASP; then the WASP made history; and now history has apparently abandoned him, has tossed him aside, and has left his fellow travelers without focus, without durable heroes, and without a common ethic. From history's pet to history's fool, he was, for three centuries, the heir of all that we regarded as most admirable, most hopeful, and most civilized in the West. Out of the particular version of the Renaissance that created the Elizabethan adventurer— entrepreneur, explorer, investor, conqueror of nature—and out of the particular version of the Reformation that created the Puritan, this country forged an ethic, an image, and a style which not only defined what we were as individuals or a nation, but came to represent (in our minds, and often in those of Europeans) the ultimate in Western possibilities.*

—PETER M. SCHRAG

2. Confessions

Glenn R. Bucher

THE WASP NEST

John Fitzgerald Kennedy's election to the presidency in 1960, and publication of Peter Schrag's *The Decline of the WASP*[1] one decade later, share a symbolic commonality. The latter, written by a straight male German-American Jew, is an effort to interpret new social phenomena, of which the former (pertaining to a straight male Irish-American Catholic) was a representation. With the inauguration of President Kennedy the country was served formal notice, the ramifications of which it had not entertained on election day. No longer was the American presidency, and the power attached to it, the exclusive possession of straight male WASPs (white Anglo-Saxon Protestants).

Prior to this event America's straight male WASPs had relin-

11

quished in part their coveted hold on American power. John F. Kennedy's ambassador father Joseph P. Kennedy, Mayor La Guardia of New York, Justice Brandeis of the Supreme Court, and others had broken some barriers. But Kennedy's presidency was a departure from this sociopolitical tokenism. It spoke to the point that straight, white, male, Anglo and/or Saxon Protestants could no longer automatically claim, via national and religious inheritances, the sole and inevitable right to control of the American establishment. The "wretched masses yearning to be free" had freed one of their own enough to crown him "Liberator." The dominance of race and sex and heterosexual preference, of course, remained untouched.

Unfortunately for America's straight male WASPs, the contemporary liberation revolution is something different. If it were merely a matter of Kennedys replacing Wilsons as president, Kissingers rather than Rusks as secretary of state, Brandeises instead of Tafts on the court, and Strausses supplanting Morgans in America's corporate world, the American way of life would be intact. WASPness, essential to this style of life, can be learned, even if one's inheritance suggests otherwise. In fact, such "up-by-the-bootstraps" successes of those who came into the world as potential WASPs, in the cultural sense, have always been allowed and applauded. They are viewed as inherent to the American dream.

For straight male WASP Americans, this dream has always constituted a sacred credo. It continues to do so, even under conditions which threaten its validity. Every American of straight male WASP orientation grows up with this dream implanted in his consciousness and gonads. It inevitably affects his behavior. From the day he goes to the school-yard marble contest with eight marbles and comes home with twelve, he knows it is true. If he went with twelve and returned with eight, he received fatherly reassurance that his plight was the result of infrequent misfortune, if in fact someone did not cheat him out of his marbles. That, or else he didn't try hard enough! This Darwinesque perspective is refined slightly as maturation reveals its many nuances. But the psychic effects are always present.

The symbolic zenith of this dream is the American presidency. Blacks, women, homosexuals, and unmelted, hyphenated Americans do not think about it. Straight white males do. Not all of them want to be president. But the prestige and power associated with the position are the envy of every properly-

socialized straight white male. The election of a non-WASP was
not a serious contradiction. It confirmed the dream about what
celebrated success can result from difficult and diligent work
against overwhelming odds.

To this account of America's social expectations and opportunities there is another contemporary side. It is why Schrag's
book, and present liberation struggles, are so important. *The
Decline of the WASP* says that those who have benefited from
this dream (or hoped to), now find it is becoming a nightmare.[2]
WASPs are on the decline because non-WASPs are rising. As
President Kennedy symbolized, though only in part, WASPs are
slowly losing their grip on American power. That is alarming.
What is more frightening is that blacks, women, and homosexuals
are moving in to take places previously reserved for straight white
males. With their emergence comes the prerogative to make and
to write history. History is beginning to expose straight white
males for what they really have been and are. As Schrag says:
"Now history has abandoned him, has tossed him aside, and has
left his fellow travelers without focus, without durable heroes,
and without a common ethic."[3] In the eyes of the world, straight
white males are passing "from history's pets to history's fools."

Evidence is abundant. Straight white males are in more trouble than WASPs thought they were in 1960. America's social
revolution is out of control. For straight white males to see that
they are on the way down the American ladder of success is no
casual discovery. This new descent, juxtaposed with the psychic
remnants of the American dream which remain in straight white
male consciousness, constitutes a contradiction of immense
proportion. These two realities, commingling in the heart, mind,
and gut of a typical straight white male in American society today, explode! They create a crisis of identity which has no
American equivalent. We are speaking of straight white males
experiencing and contemplating their own demise—standing by
while the world of their American dream is transformed into a
different world. There are crises in the WASP nest.

Straight white male confessionals which expose the existential-
ity of what it has meant and now means to be a straight white male
in America must be worked out between the Scylla of this American dream and the Charybdis of the decline of the straight white
male. The rock is atrophying; the whirlpool has become
treacherous. Even so, these are the perimeters within which
straight white male liberation needs to be considered.

THE DREAM INHERITED

Connections between straight white male identity and the American dream are intimate. One's being cannot be detached from the world view which provides meaning for it; hence, the predicament of straight white males in American society today is proportional to the demise of their dream. The new circumstances, considered alone, are difficult. What makes them catastrophic is that few people, if any, are prepared for them. For the most part, the males of whom we speak inherited the American dream in an environment pregnant with the promised fulfillment of that dream; replete with straight white male father-figures who embodied what their sons were promised. This potentiality is changing. Father-figures are now viewed in a different light. Hence, straight white males seem to have no personal history upon which to rely as a source of strength and hope in the midst of this crisis. One is tempted to regard one's past as intentional deception. History is no longer weighted on the side of straight white males. But the falsification charge is unfair to those who faithfully taught that which they firmly believed and lived. If blame for an American dream unrealized—and now unrealizable—is to be assigned, perhaps the *circumstances* in which many a dream was inherited are most vulnerable.

Consider my own history as an example. For me, the American dream was inherited in "ideal" circumstances. The scene was middle-American country: a small, central-Pennsylvania college town in the heart of middle-class life, Pennsylvania Dutch agriculture, Eisenhower Republicanism, and conservative Protestantism. It was (and still is) a quiet, peaceful town, full of citizens proud to be the people they were; happy to be living where they did; and contented with America. The community's ethos was white, Anglo-Saxon, and Protestant. No one bothered to interpret or identify dominant characteristics of life in central Pennsylvania. Everyone knew that the community was like almost all of the rest of America. What that meant was never questioned, at least not publicly. Not even the town's outstanding human exceptions bothered: two Jews, a few transient black college students, a handful of Roman Catholics, and a very small contingent of Democrats.

Middle-income home and family life formed the backbone of stability for this way of life in central Pennsylvania. Father, mother, brother, a ranch-type home, two cars, a big lawn, and an immaculately-preserved home interior constituted the immediate surroundings. The situation did not reek of materialism: prudence, rationality, and relative simplicity characterized the conditions of life. Conservative religion, Republican politics, Puritan morality, and a lifestyle marked by diligence, sobriety, and integrity were the essential ingredients of this middle-American family and home, and hosts of others.

Amidst similar circumstances, many straight white males have been socialized. What was learned is predictable. America equaled decency, opportunity, success, and affluence. These qualities of life were available and obtainable. Persons with ingenuity and perseverance knew how to procure them. Straight white males especially were impressed with the need to achieve, more by what was not said than by what was. Achievement—its possibilities and probabilities—was the central theme in a subtle, yet powerful, process of socialization. There were those who didn't make it. They were "the less fortunate" who, on a weekly basis had their plight and care continually resubmitted to God for his eternal attention. To call upon God's assistance for those in distress, however, did not suggest that one's own affluence had to be adjusted in order to provide for those who did not have enough. Once God's care had been invoked, there was no need to dwell on the matter. That he had much to do with the have's having was acknowledged: what his disposition was regarding the have-not's not having was never very clear. Of course, there was always heaven!

The American dream, though not labeled, defined, or explained as such, was transmitted in this cultural milieu. That was the experience of this—and many another—straight white male. Because the dream and the ethos mutually reinforced one another, there was no need to distinguish between them: each was living proof of the other. Consequently, the net result was an indoctrination process complete with an elaborate system of motivations, rewards, and punishments. The system was enforced at two levels: parental and social. This made it particularly effective.

One did not ask questions about the straight male WASP world view. Why? Initially, because one did not have enough perspective to entertain a critical thought. Later, because that world view was the standard against which other realities could be measured. The WASP dream was a given, compatible with the world's metaphysic and God's intentions. This was what reality looked like. There was no need to question it.

Inheriting this dream had an incalculable impact upon one's

self-perceptions as a straight white male of Anglo-Saxon Protestant heritage, and on the role of these servants of God in his
world. It could not have been otherwise. That was the intent of
passing on the inheritance. What a straight white male learned
was that whiteness and maleness and heterosexual preferences
are human attributes of the first order, comparable to none. The
world was a playground for those straight white males willing to
use it as such. WASP qualities of life were essential to the development and survival of the nation and world. It was made
clear that, through ideas expressed and life lived, straight white
males were called to greatness on their own and others' behalf.

Since the American dream was about and for straight white
males, those who qualified as such could only be delighted about
the prospects promised them. Because whiteness and maleness
and heterosexual preference were the primary qualifications of
those who shaped and controlled collective social life, each
straight white male was led to believe in the potential of his own
future. If one followed the prescribed do's and don'ts, there was
no reason to doubt the imminence of success. But this dream
also functioned as a nightmare for those whose persons and destinies fell outside the dream's promises. Blacks, women, and
homosexuals were all incorporated into this prevailing ideology,
but in destructive ways. Unfortunately, straight white males acquired prejudices and stereotypes which are not easily forgotten.

The images are familiar. Black was engrained as a negative
linguistic symbol, as evidenced by black book, black sheep, and
black lie. It also referred to a group of people (though "Negro"
was preferred) characterized as shiftless, lazy, emotional, smelly,
and intellectually inferior. There were positive racist stereotypes, too: blacks could sing, dance, run, and fornicate with authority. They were to be feared; they were after what straight
white males had. They were "the Other." They were different.
They lived where they did because they failed to do anything to
get themselves out of the human mess they were in. Proof of that
were the tokens who made it and who received constant attention
as those Negroes who had realized the American dream. Tokens
confirmed the theory: the dream was for all. It allowed individual worth to surface. At the universal level, blacks were
equal. It was only in specific cases that they were not.

Women fared no differently, except in detail. In fact, the images here were stronger because middle-American housewives fit
so well the stereotypes passed on about them, whereas most

families were not immediately in touch with blacks. What little boys learned about women they could observe daily, usually in their own homes. Women were sensitive and compassionate; docile and obedient. The roles of housewife and mother necessitated these qualities; the qualities pointed to the roles they legitimatized. Women were intended *by nature* to be in the service of their husbands and children. Most were. They enjoyed a special place in the straight white male world—at one and the same time secondary, and yet the embodiment of necessary attributes which only they could manifest. Female images which straight white males inherited proved to legitimatize not only the role of woman, but also that of her male "head."

The American dream dispensed in central Pennsylvania included very little about homosexuality. Sex was not a popular topic and there were many taboos connected with discussing it. Heterosexual preference was assumed to be the only comprehensible mode. The facts of life were, though somewhat embarrassingly, discussed with male peers. They had usually to do with the female reproductive systems and the emotional ramifications of sex. Straight white males learned early what they still believe: when it comes to sex, that is a feminine matter. Somehow, males don't need any information about themselves. It is understandable why homosexuality was scarcely mentioned, and then only in judgmental ways. One had heard of "fairies" and "queers." They were freaks who, basically sick, could be helped with therapy or medicine. At no time was the notion entertained that homosexuality was a sexual preference legitimate for some.

These were the circumstances and dream to which this straight white male was exposed from the beginning. Three conclusions are worth noting: (1) straight white males have come to believe strongly in their whiteness and maleness and heterosexuality through their environmental socialization; (2) in the midst of severe identity crises straight white males have difficulty returning to their personal and social histories for support and hope; (3) it is understandable, therefore, why straight white males find the option of cursing their pasts so attractive. It is with a response to the cursing that we must complete this account.

Some who have recently ventured descriptions of American *rites de passage* have committed a regrettable error. The politicized sons and daughters of Middle America have *denounced* their parents. Jerry Rubin, for example, urged middle-class youth to "bring the war home: kill your parents."[4] Straight white males, who have discovered that their parents and relatives were involved in the guilt of their culture rather than being the epitome of humanity, have been inclined to dismiss good parental intentions in an act of outraged moral disbelief.

Nothing similar to that response is intended in the foregoing account. In an important article, "The Great White Son Turns Left," E. Gordon Dalbey, Jr. speaks eloquently, though chauvinistically, to the point that must be emphasized:

> Instead of cursing our fathers, we white youth must begin to build upon the history they have given us, to redeem their uncompleted manhood. This is what sons are for. We will want our own sons to do the same for us—though we shall greet their discovery of our incompleteness with joy. The revolutionary task of our time is not to reject one's parents, or indeed to forgive them. Rather, the task is to forgive oneself for having loved one's parents as a child, so that one can begin to love as an adult.[5]

Consciousness and ideology, initially, are inheritances of circumstances over which one has only *ex post facto* control. But the mature identity struggle is incomplete without a perspective on those circumstances and, therefore, an analysis of the impact they have upon one's being. Such a coming-to-terms necessitates forgiveness and the building of the future together. To reflect critically on the inheriting of a dream is to work at forgiving and to hope for building.

To receive or not to receive the American dream is not an option for most straight white males born in America. This was true in the 1940s and 1950s; it is still true, though the circumstances in middle America, and consequently its world view, are somewhat different. Having received the dream, the task is rather to come to conscious awareness of what that dream is and how it has neatly honed straight white males to fit the American system. That growing awareness is a function of time. The time is now!

But there are choices, extremely important ones. To adopt uncritically *or* to analyze thoroughly that which one has inherited, and consequently is, constitutes one choice. An equally radical choice is to begin to understand the ideological American dream and its implications in the context of those who have been abused by it *or* to refuse to see it in that context. Who one is to become as a straight white male has much to do with the choices one makes.

THE DREAM CHALLENGED

With the outset of World War I, progressivism and social gospel Christianity—precursors to the liberalism of the 1960s—suffered a severe setback. In 1932 Reinhold Niebuhr, recognizing liberalism's bankruptcy and the preposterous moral claims that American educators were making about their impact on social morality, warned in *Moral Man and Immoral Society:*

> A careful study of the history of political and economic life proves conclusively that the educators, as all other middle-class moralists, underestimate the conflict of interest in political and economic relations, and attribute to disinterested ignorance what ought usually to be attributed to interested intelligence.[6]

That education had a cause-effect relationship with morality seemed to him dubious, for those who are knowledgeable often employ their skills in the service of narrow self-interest.

Three decades after Niebuhr wrote these words the inherited American dream of this straight white male was challenged by my graduate education in religion. But it was only *challenged*—which bears out Niebuhr's judgment. Perhaps that is all middle-class education can ever be, given the dominant cultural values which pervade educational institutions. That is all it did, in any event, to my inherited world view.

The shift of educational locus from a "small Christian college" (which produced small Christians) to well-known liberal, urban, Protestant graduate schools was bound to have its effects, even if they were not radical. That was the case as, intent upon enjoying the success that my personal American dream had urged and guaranteed, I set out upon a course of doctoral study. The objective, though distant, was clear: to be an influential and prominent professor in mainline American society.

Survival in the urbanity of New York and Boston was itself an educational experience. Dualities of power and powerlessness, wealth and poverty, white and blacks, WASPs and ethnics, love and hate, peace and violence, and sophisticated culture and its antithesis came to life amidst the hustle and dirt of the city. It was one experience to read about America's cultural pluralism, another to be confronted with it. Apart from formal academia, these experiences challenged the particulars of the inherited American dream.

The cultural pluralism of urban life was a familiar concept, but it had never been experienced in the Pennsylvania setting where cultural and racial conformity prevailed. Pluralism was a theoretical aspect of the inherited dream: America was the place where the individuality of non-WASPs lost its offensive edges while nonetheless remaining intact. In America, one could become a WASP and still be an individual, according to the dream. As was the case with much of that theoretical dream, however, it failed to capture and to communicate what actually happened to all those immigrants who did not swiftly make it into the open arms of the great middle class, thereby losing their edges.

Urban existence exposed this reality gap. Black and ethnic neighborhoods were not simply colored, urban versions of typical communities, central-Pennsylvania style. They had a distinctive character: one molded by conflicts between the need to conform and the inability to do so. Unlike what the dream suggested, it was evident that something was awry with the melting process. Some never got to the pot: the invitation was not open-ended. Others did not melt, either because they couldn't or wouldn't. The salvific qualities ascribed to middle-classness were not universally available: that socioeconomic status was intended for some, and not others. The society was making a decision about who could enter and who could not.

Urban neighborhoods, though, symbolized more than the inadequacies of the American dream. They were also communities which performed powerful and essential psychosocial functions for those who, for some reason or other, did not move to Long Island. They constituted the world for those who lived therein, and provided the concrete shape around which one's view of the world molded. There was a racial and cultural integrity present which the American dream disregarded and abused. Some did not want to abandon their cultural identity to become WASPs.

These were the surroundings in which this straight white male's American dream was challenged. There were other more specific and personal realities, too. With the beginning of graduate study a transition had been made from suburban middle America to the world of the urban middle class. That describes the social ethos of the graduate schools, of course, and not the neighborhoods in which they were located. It also characterizes the colleagues and professors with whom one was surrounded, and the fashionable Madison Avenue Presbyterian Church in which field education was pursued.

As intimate encounters occurred in these settings, adjustments took place. Ambitions, priorities, and goals were called into

question; they were reevaluated. Inevitably, one's world view
and understanding of American society changed. Self changed.
One began to regret one's past as a new future unfolded. On
reflection, one's background seemed deprived, unsophisticated,
and limited and limiting. Power and prestige took on new meaning as one encountered those straight white males who had done
precisely what the dream prescribed. Becoming a professional
member of the *real* establishment emerged as a desirable goal.
Two matters were clear: that objective was still attainable, because there was proof of it; and given the late start this straight
white male had up the long American road to success, energetic
hard work was a vital virtue.

The most profound challenges during graduate school took
place at the theological level since that was what my educational
adventure was all about. Conservative religion, though obviously modified by college, still lingered in heart and mind. It was
characterized by personalism, pietism, evangelicalism, sectarianism, legalism, and pacifism. In a liberal Protestant setting,
these were challenged and changed, due to the nature of theological inquiry, but also because one's newly determined social aspi-
rations did not fit with the religion of past days.

A strong prophetic religion and social activism displaced personalism. Pietism came to be viewed as self-righteous. In its
stead a healthy set of enjoyable sins developed, for which one
constantly needed forgiveness. Evangelicalism was too rigid for
the tolerance that social pluralism required; an open-ended uni-
versalism replaced it. Sectarianism for upper-middle-class Protestants was simply not an option: it failed to take seriously the
social responsibility one exercised as a social change agent. Regarding religious legalisms, they were unbiblical, imperiled with
"holier than thou" overtones; to be legalistic was to be more
certain than anyone could be about the nature of religious faith.

Pacifism was a story in itself. From historical origins of conservative religion arose a strong commitment to pacifism, both in
personal and social life. Though few members of my hometown
church were in positions (with the government or the military for
example) where that commitment was challenged, a belief that
one should be uncompromising in his/her allegiance to it was
held. It was clear that such views were difficult to practice.
Pacifism was one of those "impossible possibilities" which provided a theoretical ideal toward which an individual and a society
could move. It was assumed that nothing in the essential Ameri-

can social fabric contradicted the realization of the ideal. If the nation worked harder at peace, pacifism would be the result. It was the impossibility of the ideal to which one witnessed.

These pacifist views, still held in modified form, were seriously questioned within a liberal Protestant seminary where the Christian political realism of Reinhold Niebuhr and John C. Bennett prevailed. In that place during World War II, great debates ensued regarding the question of personal commitment to America's war involvement. Human scars created by the developing consensus around "Christian" responsibility to participate in that war had not healed altogether. It is understandable, then, why a young, somewhat naïve, pacifist would be greeted with disbelief and challenge.

The matter of participation in war, however, was not the only issue at stake. Pacifism and sectarianism fit together. One could be a vocational pacifist if he/she had little responsibility for, or interest in, the establishment. Upper-middle-class graduate students, already a part of that order (if vicariously, only through their fathers) were not able to understand how a responsible member of society could insist that the country assume a pacifistic stance in light of its needs for national security. That the nation could never take on such a character, given the immorality of nation states, was a given. These arguments were personally compelling. One had to acknowledge that the pacifist position was not for those liberals (one of whom I had now become) burdened with tasks of righting wrongs in society as realistically as possible. To change with regard to pacifism was to remove one of the remaining contradictions between my religion and my new way of life.

These years were characterized by a challenging liberalization of the inherited American dream. It was obvious that the social goodies of the original dream were far more difficult for some to acquire than had been previously supposed. The obstacles—in many cases, the impossibilities—were great, through no fault of those involved. Liberalism dramatically portrayed the corruption of society; it also held tenaciously to the view that the nation could deliver on the dream it promised. Although some social matters were out of joint, with Band-Aids and other patchwork the true essence of American society could be realized.

The conservative dream of central Pennsylvania was challenged by the liberalism of graduate education in urban America. The vision of a virtuous society gave way to that of an unjust, though potentially redeemable, society. The mythology about pots of gold at the ends of aspiring immigrants' rainbows succumbed to the realities of urban life. A straight white male dream, the world view which it presupposed, and the social goals advanced were transformed into a realistic assessment of the modest possibilities and complex limitations of the social order. Charles A. Reich accurately described the result in *The Greening of America:*

> Consciousness II believes that the present American crisis can be solved by greater commitment of individuals to the public interest, more social responsibility by private business, and above all, by more affirmative government action—regulation, planning, more of a welfare state, better and more rational administration and management.[7]

The new insight that the society was far more corrupt than had been supposed led to the conclusion that the reformation of it would require more zealous commitment from those heretofore assured of inheriting it.

Liberalism did not alter the inherited stature of whiteness and maleness. That straight males of WASP orientation bore some of the responsibility for the unhealthy condition of the nation-state was evident. That what they could expect to find in mainstream America was less wholesome than anticipated was apparent, too. That they needed to work for reform was undeniable. What is important to note is that the special privilege and favor afforded straight white males remained intact and beyond question. There was racism in America. No one spoke of sexism. And though homosexuality surfaced now and again in graduate school, no one was actually prepared to ask questions about the nature of sexual preferences. All this meant that the essential wholeness of America's society would be fulfilled when straight white males instituted necessary adjustments.

The Dream Destroyed

The year was 1968. Ten years of post-secondary education, a privilege available to energetic and compulsive straight white males of WASP disposition, culminated in the oft-coveted doctor of philosophy degree. In this male's guts there was the need to succeed; in the heart, a desire to set aright an America gone astray. Liberal political philosophy and strategies of social change consistent with it were the means by which the restoration would be accomplished. The next step up the long road to

straight white male fulfillment was obvious: a job. Days of learning were over, years of productive contributions about to com-
mence. Within this context, then, this newly qualified professor
of social ethics accepted a teaching position at the school of religion of a predominantly black university. Why? Fundamentally,
because racism was rampant in America. It would be eliminated
as well-intentioned straight white males assisted blacks in their
struggle for justice. Or so it seemed.

The times were catastrophic. That only accentuated the validity of my decision. The assassinations of Martin Luther King, Jr.
and Robert F. Kennedy; urban riots; expanded war in Southeast
Asia; the Democratic Convention of 1968; and the election of
Richard M. Nixon—all of these and more were outrageous af-
fronts to the liberal mind. To comprehend the times, interpretations developed which legitimatized the liberal world view. Society, far from the virtuous bulwark which its newly-elected President affirmed it to be, had taxed the limits of its recoverable
ability. Only a monumental commitment to such liberal causes
as civil rights, peace, and election reform could save the nation
from itself. The latter days of 1968 seemed like auspicious times
for straight white male liberals with vision. Blacks and other
debtors awaited efforts at social reconstruction.

What happened at that time and in these circumstances is that
which this chapter and this book are about. The facts cry out for
exposure; they are a necessary preface to the matter of liberation.
The setting was an alien one—a member of the white minority on
a university faculty at a predominantly black, Freedman's-
Bureau-created university. There were a few whites (all males)
and orientals amidst the black student body. Because my wife
and I were "committed," a decision was made to live within close
proximity to the university. The neighborhood was black,
though the condominium in which we lived was predominantly
white. The city's population was 75 percent black, whereas the
public schools in which my wife taught were 90 percent black.
The circumstances were both threatening and ideal: the former
because we were strangers in a strange land; the latter because it
was a white liberal paradise. There was so much to do!

Clearly defined tasks emerged in the black community. The
education of blacks was important. Through the relatively im-
partial medium of education, they could succeed in mainstream
America. To participate in the black fight for social justice was
also a commitment. The urban riots of 1968 made it clear that the

"civil rights struggle" was not over. For a white liberal who presumably understood the corruptions and possibilities of the American system, it was appropriate to share that wisdom with blacks. To witness in the white community to the fact that racism still existed was a final responsibility. The anticipated results were twofold: (1) that well-meaning whites would be overwhelmed by the prevalence of social racism and injustice; and (2) that many whites would, as in the case of the civil rights events in the mid and late sixties, still join the quest for freedom.

Behind these notions lay classic liberal assumptions: American society was essentially just, potentially if not actually. To be middle-class American was what everyone wanted and needed to be. Almost all—via hard work, public and private assistance, opportunism, and luck—could enjoy relative success in the society. Education remained an important and legitimate medium for social advancement; its relative "neutrality" was worth preserving for black self-fulfillment. Finally, this agenda assumed that middle-class whites were prepared to understand the insidious dimensions of personal and social racism, and to risk some of their welfare in behalf of its elimination.

That these tasks, and their undergirding world view were about to be relegated to the status of ideology (a rationalization for the status quo), just as had the inherited American dream before, soon became evident. A series of dramatic events shattered this not-so-realistic realism beyond recognition. Consequently, the two-year professorship and stay in this alien setting proved to be the most significant period of this straight white male's intellectual and emotional life. The conclusion was soon obvious: the liberal world view, not unlike its more conservative antecedent, was at drastic variance with social realities. That being the case, the moral clout of liberalism was somewhat defunct.

The realities were these: Black male graduate students, products of America's public schools and colleges, could neither read nor write as well as middle-class white junior high school students. Many worked for meager wages at meaningless jobs eight hours a day in order to attend graduate school. Often, by age twenty-two they had been married, become parents, been divorced, and remarried. By their own admission, many needed psychiatric assistance to deal with collapsed self-images. More than a few had been consumed by a subculture of poverty, depression, disease, and despair. Though they had shaken some of this, the results were still apparent. For some—these were graduate students in theology, remember—life seemed to have lost hope if, in fact, it had ever had any. The scene was grim.

Beyond academia the evidence was different though corroborative: Black inner-city neighborhoods gutted by fire and filth; groups of black men aimlessly wandering the streets in search of work or food; a steady diet of violence and death on the block; police brutality and corruption; hospital clinics and emergency rooms packed with black women and children in search either of a needed doctor or of a roof over their heads; two black custodians at our predominantly white condominium whose living quarters were terribly inadequate, whose constant inebriation was interrupted only now and then by work; a general poverty of life and spirit. These were realities, too!

Psychologically, emotionally, and intellectually, life for a straight white male of liberal WASP orientation was hell amidst these daily obscenities. To be part of a racial minority in an alien world dominated by unfamiliar realities turns one's being upside down. The matter of personal identity, never even an issue before, suddenly became paramount. Paranoia about personal safety was a concern. One felt trapped in a situation which he could do nothing about. The daily anxieties about things important and inconsequential became consuming. In the smallest of ways, one began to sense the torture and anguish with which blacks and other minorities have lived in America. There were two differences, however: (1) blacks do not have the option of leaving alien America; and (2) America is not a black world and Africa, for most, is not their home. And they cannot afford a psychiatrist!

These experiences destroyed the liberalism of this straight white male. That a society alleged to be essentially just and potentially sound could ignore and thereby tolerate these conditions was an absurdity, particularly when it was that society which created the conditions. Liberalism failed to recognize the horror of the system in which it believed so much and worked so diligently to improve. The liberals of the sixties, however "radical" they thought they were, had not really understood the dimensions of the social problem, in part because they didn't want to. Because they continued to benefit from the social arrangements which relegated blacks to these desperate conditions, it was in their self-interest *not* to comprehend in more than the most superficial ways.

In *For Whites Only*, Robert W. Terry captures the white liberal dilemma which became so apparent:

> Efforts to overcome alienation by assimilating blacks into the mainstream of American life have presupposed the mainstream as the desirable standard. Equality with whites is the goal. What the liberal does not understand is that equality with whites is a racist goal. Why should blacks want to be equal to white racists?[8]

That says it. Mainstream America is polluted. Structural and institutional racism exist. Liberalism did not and does not reflect a complete understanding of the nature of social injustice. Middle-class straight white male liberals are caught in a no-exit hypocrisy; one cannot be part of mainstream America *and* committed to changing it. That is contradictory; the necessary changes will inevitably jeopardize one's own social standing. Liberals seem unwilling to risk that.

WHAT NEXT?

The dream, liberal though it was, disintegrated in the face of facts. According to the liberal ideology, straight white males were the creators, maintainers, and change agents of the American way of life. To the extent that the mainstream required pollution control, those were enviable tasks. When it became apparent that the bed of the stream was rotten, that implicated straight white males in a different way. They were structurally involved in the rottenness. Finally it was clear: racism is a white, not a black, problem. The energy of white liberals had been expended in the wrong place. If racism is a white problem, then it must be exposed and remedied in the white community, where it is. That is where I promptly went, and somewhat reluctantly remain. Two discoveries have occurred since my arrival: (1) the discovery that all along I had not just been a white, but a *straight* white *male*; and (2) the discovery that, contrary to my expectations, Middle America has no intention of giving up its racism—or its chauvinism or its sexism.

NOTES

*Peter Schrag, *The Decline of the WASP* (New York: Simon & Schuster, 1971), p. 70.

1. Schrag, *Decline of the WASP*.
2. Ibid., p. 17.

3. Ibid., p. 14.

4. Gordon Dalbey, Jr., "The Great White Son Turns Left," *The Christian Century*, 88, no. 23 (June 9, 1971):716.

5. Ibid., p. 719.

6. Reinhold Niebuhr, *Moral Man and Immoral Society* (New York: Charles Scribner's Sons, 1932), p. 215.

7. Charles A. Reich, *The Greening of America* (New York: Random House, 1970), p. 66.

8. Robert W. Terry, *For Whites Only* (Grand Rapids: Eerdmans, 1970), p. 55.

Part Two

From the Slaves:
To the Masters

We have become unbelievers, no longer believing in the absolute superiority of the white man's juju. You have never practiced what you preached. Why should we believe in you?
Why would we want to be like you?*

—John O. Killens

3.   Black Power and Straight White Males

Benjamin D. Berry

Several years ago, Julius Lester issued a warning to white
America: "Look Out Whitey! Black Power's Gonna Git Your
Momma." Had I been writing about that time (1968), I would
have sounded much the same warning. Those were the years of
radical rhetoric, violent action, and burning cities. Black power
as a slogan, an idea, and a movement had unceremoniously
shoved the more passive Civil Rights movement from center
stage. Without the courtesy of a warning to white America, a new
brand of black male and female leadership emerged to take the
place of the accepted King-Wilkins-Young group. Black women
threw away their straightening combs; black men shed the Madison Avenue look; and the fierce Black Panther glared from almost
every wall in the black ghetto.

I recall those days for two very simple reasons: First they are
gone, and you, dear reader, in the quiet of the present moment
may have already forgotten them; Americans, especially white
Americans, have unbelievably short memories when it comes to
black folk. And secondly, I recall those days because the outward and visible changes of the late 1960s mask a more radical
and lasting change in black America which white America has
never seen. It is another peculiar failing of the white American

30

version of the human being that it fails to look beneath the surface of anything. It has refused to see this recent change in blacks just as it earlier refused to see the cancer in the nation that was slavery. The fact is that white is not right; it is *blind!* So, for the benefit of what I assume to be a predominantly white readership, let me return now to the days of yesteryear, and bring to your vision some very important truths.

BLACK POWER AS A NEW COSMOLOGY

In the midst of the "rap" of H. Rap Brown, the Mau-Mauing of Stokely Carmichael, and the guns of Huey Newton, a new world view was forming in the dark ghettos of America. This nation's history may be written as that of one group's (straight white male) efforts to control the decision-making process, and therefore the destinies, of all other groups. The straight white male related to blacks as the self-proclaimed superior being. He believed his superiority included areas of the intellect, physical prowess, sexual stamina, and morality. He codified this superiority in legal and social structures. An address to the United States Senate by James Vardaman, Senator from the state of Mississippi (1911–19), reflects that ideology:

> The door of hope might have remained closed so far as the progress the negro (sic.) was to make for himself was concerned. He has never created for himself any civilization. He has never risen above the government of a club. He has never written a language. His achievements in architecture are limited to the thatched-roofed hut or a hole in the ground. No monuments have been builded by him to body forth and perpetuate in the memory of posterity the virtues of his ancestors. . . . In truth, he has never progressed, save and except when under the influence and absolute control of a superior race.[1]

In spite of the rhetoric, the actions of the straight white male seemed to betray a certain fear that all was not as he claimed it to be. The vaunted superiority was not securely embedded even in his own mind, and he feared that future generations would allow it to slip through their grasp. He therefore built a philosophy into the educational system to insure that his progeny would continue it. Both black and white children to this day study the glorious deeds of the white founding fathers. Thus, white supremacy has become an integral part of the American cosmology, along with manifest destiny, free enterprise, and apple pie.

Although this was a cosmology created by white men for the benefit of white men, many blacks, and almost all white women, came to accept it as reality. Indeed, there was evidence all around to support the white claim to superiority. White wealth, white beauty, white culture were not only dominant, but the standards by which all else was judged. Thus, the nappy hair, the broad nose, the thick lips of the black person, being the antithesis of white characteristics, were ugly. Some blacks—at the time the vast majority of blacks—underwent much physical pain in a futile attempt, not to be *like* white people, but to *be* white. And, as this is a physical impossibility, a certain psychopathology developed in which the black person became a non-person. Franz Fanon describes it this way:

> When the Negro makes contact with the white world, a certain sensitizing action takes place. If his psychic structure is weak, one observes a collapse of the ego. The black man stops behaving as an *actional* person. The goal of his behavior will be The Other (in the guise of the white man), for The Other alone can give him worth.[2]

Robert Coles graphically portrayed how black children in the South lost all respect for themselves and their kin at an early age because of the constant humiliation which they suffered, and, more importantly, which they were forced to witness in their parents who had no capacity to fight back.[3]

We see, then, that accompanying the concept of white superiority was the companion concept of black inferiority. From the very document which gives life to this nation, to the picture of the founder of the religion to which most of us adhere, it is the unchallenged power of the white male over black persons and property that lies at the root of the society. The black person, especially the black male, felt the weight of his lowly status on a daily basis. He was forced to address white children as adults, while they spoke to him, if at all, as a child. None of the avenues of American mobility was open to him—not even crime, for he was doomed to stealing from his own poor people. In American society, the black man was an animal or a beast. He was feared by some, hated by others, but always controlled. In this peculiar cosmology, the black man functioned as a fixed star. He would always be there to serve as the bottom of the socioeconomic-political pyramid. All else might change, but "niggers will always be niggers."

It is a mark of the blindness of white people that, at least until very recently, they believed that black people enjoyed this situation. They are still hard-pressed to understand why, after all they have done for us, we are not content with our station in life. In the 1960s, when the Civil Rights movement was in full swing, many would come to us and ask: "What do you people want?" The black man who replied, "What have you got?" was a smart nigger. Nor could whites cope with the very factual statement, "Get your foot off my neck." For they could see neither the foot nor the neck held so securely under it.

At the root of the Civil Rights movement was the demand for integration. We might date the beginning of that movement with the successful fight for a court ruling in favor of school desegregation, for it was that success that gave impetus to the sit-ins and demonstrations that were to follow. At first the movement was met with clubs, dogs, hoses, and the twisted face of hate. Integration was anathema south of the "Cotton Curtain." George Wallace stood his little body in the schoolhouse door. Clement Hainsworth "out-niggered" his opponents. And Lester Maddox sold axe handles with which his friends and neighbors could whip niggers' heads. It is an interesting commentary on the state of white society that that schoolhouse door opened for Wallace paths toward presidential candidacy! Hainsworth was nominated for the Supreme Court; and Maddox was elected governor. Obviously, whites who shout "nigger" the loudest can still succeed in this nation.

The flaw that killed the Civil Rights movement was that those young blacks who filled the streets and jails of the South—and I was among them—were, in effect, confirming the view of the universe that white men had created. We were attempting to join white America. We were marching and singing in an effort to live next door, go to the same schools, use the same toilets—be white! And we wanted it badly enough to die for it! And many did die: too many! But the universe did not change. White was still enthroned.

The price of joining white America, when it allowed a few of us to pass through the veil, was the denial of our blackness, which is to say, a denial of ourselves, for a man cannot be what he is not. No amount of bleaching cream or education or proper language is able to change a black man into a white man. It was a futile hope held out to a few blacks by white liberals who, in the guise of support for the movement, sought to strengthen their hold on their superior status.

But history marches on. A suppressed people will not stand still forever. On the streets of the ghetto, and in those dark

nightspots in Harlem which saw a white face only under the cloak
of night, lay the roots of a revolution which was to emerge in the
fiery nights of Newark and Detroit and almost every major city in
this nation. In what has come to be known as the "language of
soul"; in the music which blacks have long appreciated but
whites have only recently discovered; in the noisy churches with
emotional preachers and more emotional women; in the messages
of Coltrane, Bird, and Ray Charles lay an appreciation, no, a *love*
of blackness that was to shake the foundation of the straight white
male's universe and cause a cataclysmic event that for him
closely resembled the prophesy of the Book of Revelation:

> Behold, there was a great earthquake; and the sun became black
> as sackcloth, the full moon became like blood and the stars of
> the sky fell to the earth as the fig tree sheds its winter fruit when
> shaken by a gale; the sky vanished like a scroll that is rolled up,
> and every mountain and island was removed from its place.[4]

Black power dealt a terrific blow to the straight white male
ego. Couched in those two awesome words was a rejection of
everything white people had determined to be good and true and
beautiful. Openly, blacks praised their blackness, their kinky
hair, broad noses, and thick lips. Black women, once thought to
be below white women, were elevated to the pinnacle. But, true
to form, whites were unable to see behind the symbols. Black
power meant the emergence of a new universe in which, to use
Fanon's terms, the first were last and the last first. It was the
beginning of the process of American decolonization!

It is true that black power did not alter the world politically,
economically, or socially. Straight white males continued to sit
in the seats of power and control the wealth. The decision-
making machinery was still in white hands. But, psychologically, the straight white male can no longer feel secure in his
position, and that insecurity is tearing him apart. The new consciousness in the black people of this land has not been matched
by a new consciousness in the white male, though it has some
contemporary parallels in the white female.

Much of the anguish and anxiety of the situation exploded in
the political arena in 1968. Nixon, Agnew, and Wallace were the
benefactors of a futile attempt to force the universe back into the
old mold. This three-headed monster represented the white reaction to the black challenge. The rhetoric of law and order trans-
lated into a violent statement of racial superiority and determina-
tion to employ the power of the state to preserve the rightful place

of straight white males at the top of humanity. At no time did any one of the three heads use racial terms (and that was a miracle for Wallace). But only the most naïve could mistake what was being said. "Crime in the streets" meant niggers in the streets; "restore law and order" meant putting the niggers back in their place.

The political victories of 1968 were not as sweet as Nixon and his ilk had expected. Mr. Nixon, as the nation watched in amazement, fell victim to his own greed. He became the first president in history to resign under pressure. But, he did quiet the ghettos and stop the rioting that marked the late sixties. For all practical purposes, the Black Power movement died during the Nixon years, for, like the Civil Rights movement before it, black power needed victories and at least vigorous if not violent resistance in order to live. The policy of "benign neglect" was successful in stilling the raging beast that had been unleashed in the ghettos of America.

Although the movement is dead, one look at the streets of the major U.S. cities, the halls of the state and national legislatures, and the ivy-covered classrooms of American academe will let any observant person know that the universe has not been pushed back into pre-1960s order. In places where a few years ago no black could be found, a few now sit. In places where a few were found, many now stand. The situation, far from ideal, gives some indication of what can be expected in the decade ahead.

BLACK AND WHITE IN THE DECADE AHEAD

Many thoughtful people look back on the 1963 book of James Baldwin, *The Fire Next Time,* as being terribly prophetic of what was to transpire in this nation.[5] It became obvious in the so-called riots that followed the publication of that book that Baldwin was indeed a prophet. Even the spokesman of nonviolence, Dr. Martin Luther King, Jr., began to sound as if one more defeat for his method would result in his turning to a philosophy of at least self-defense for black people. I am sure that those in the seats of power did not want that man, with his remarkable capacity to move masses of humanity to action, to take that turn. Many of us, looking at the moment with myopic vision, wrote and spoke in those days of the coming revolution, much as Paul had written of the Second Coming. But, as with Paul and the Parousia, our change did not come, at least not as we (Paul and the rest of us) had expected it.

If there was/is a black revolution it has taken/is taking place in the minds of black people, and has not yet reached the streets and institutions of the land. Carmichael and Hamilton argued that black people need to define *themselves* in ways which will free them from the yoke of oppression:

> We shall have to struggle for the right to create our own terms through which to define ourselves and our relationship to the society, and to have these terms recognized. This is the first necessity of a free people, and the first right that any oppressor must suspend.[6]

What occurred in the 1960s was the beginning of this process: black people defining for themselves who they are. For straight white males, it was obvious that this meant natural hair and African clothes. True to form the masters and their economic system of exploitative capitalism sought to reap the benefits of these visible changes. Within six months after African garb became popular in the black community, it was available through the Sears Catalog and, for those handy with a sewing machine, Simplicity patterns. Within two months of the film *Superfly*'s effect on the dress patterns of *some* black males, J. C. Penney's had an entire wardrobe available. In the mind of the straight white male, any effort by blacks to liberate their minds should mean increased profits for the captains of the commercial arena.

But the black revolution did/does not stop at the outward and visible symbols of blackness. It is a revolution that involves the casting off of the values of white society (along with the symbols of white society), and the creating of a new set of black values. There is reason to hope that these new values will show a higher level of appreciation for humanity than have the materialistic-individualistic values of decadent white America. The black revolution is one of black people working to build "community" in the midst of a society that despises the word.

Philip Slater gives a somewhat more concise picture of the value structure which the black revolution rejects. He says that the basic human desires for community, engagement, and dependence are frustrated by the fundamental aspects of white American culture and its commitment to the value of individualism. The more independent Americans become, the more they feel "disconnected, bored, lonely, unprotected, unnecessary, and unsafe."[7]

It is significant that many blacks are turning to Africa and to Africans for intellectual stimulation and self-definition. While black Americans are not Africans, we are an African people who have little relation to the America created by the straight white male. Our acculturation has not been accompanied by structural assimilation, i.e., a black man who wears a Brooks Brothers suit, has a hair cut, speaks perfect English, and has a Ph.D is still a nigger anywhere in this country. African cultural concepts are aiding black Americans in the search for themselves and their community. When seen in light of the African heritage, cultural aspects of the black community which had been the brunt of jokes and slurs take on new and enriched meaning. One such cultural trait that undergoes reinterpretation is that of male dress. Whites (and some blacks) have traditionally looked upon the distinctive dress of the ghetto male as a mark of a lack of sophistication. However, Paul Harrison gives a new vision of the brother in light of African philosophy:

> Clothes are not worn simply to cover the body; they are designed by the wearer to affect a magical attitude. And the colors are not designed to be simply LOUD AND STRONG: shine is important, not brightness. . . . It's all about power; when one hits the turbulence of the streets, one must know before passing the door of the house that one's magic is complete.[8]

The significant point here is that blacks are *not* looking to the straight white male as a model for dress, behavior, or values. They are looking elsewhere. In the years ahead it will increasingly be this phenomenon that will shape the relations between the races in this nation. Blacks will continue to refuse assimilation into the polluted mainstream of American society. How whites, and straight white males in particular, respond to that rejection will be the crucial question of the decade ahead. Thus far, the response to the liberating activities of nonwhites throughout the world has been frightening. From the slaughter of Far Eastern crusades-to-save-capitalism to the threats of annihilation aimed at Middle Eastern oil producers, the straight white male is demonstrating his inability to accept the new equality—an equality which he did not grant but which has been thrust upon him by those he once oppressed.

In 1904, W.E.B. DuBois wrote that the problem of the twentieth century would be the problem of the color line.[9] Even then Dr. DuBois gave that question international significance, and the truth of his statement is becoming increasingly clear today. Black power is but one aspect of a rising consciousness in non-white peoples of their right to self-determination. That this is a drastic change in the universe as whites have known it is an understatement. If the straight white male does not change his values and his behavior to match the changes taking place in the world around him, he will not survive.

In the aftermath of the black power years, few blacks are terribly concerned about what happens to whites and the society they have created. Many of us are elated to see the Arabs "doin' they thang." We were quietly rooting for the Viet Cong. But, like it or not, our destinies are, at the moment, bound to those of white Americans. My fear is that, as the straight white male falls from his pinnacle of power, he will use the technology he has developed and the power he has amassed to take the rest of humanity with him. Nuclear holocaust IS POSSIBLE. Therefore, until we either get our five states (a la The Honorable Elijah Mohammed), go to Africa (not *back* to Africa), or in some other manner divest ourselves of this society, it is in our own interest to help the straight white male liberate himself from himself.

Black power grew out of the failure of integration, a failure caused by the demand that black people deny their blackness in order to become a part of the American society. James Baldwin, in that same prophetic book, redefined integration in a manner that might rescue the straight white male from himself:

> If the word *integration* means anything, this is what it means: that we, with love, shall force our [white] brothers to see themselves as they are, to cease fleeing from reality and begin to change it.[10]

White society has not accepted that definition of integration, as the continuing clashes over school populations graphically demonstrate. We do not want your daughters, white America! Your death grip on the past has driven out whatever love there was in us. Black people must also reject that definition of integration, at least until whites come to the realization that black liberation is the only hope left for America. It is only as *we* are free, dear reader, that *you* will become free.

NOTES

*John O. Killens, *Black Man's Burden* (New York: Simon & Schuster, Trident Press, 1965).

1. James K. Vardaman before the United States Senate, February 6, 1914, as quoted in Leslie H. Fishel, Jr. and Benjamin Quarles, *The*

Negro American: A Documentary History (Glenview, Ill.: Scott, Foresman & Co., 1967), p. 387.

2. Franz Fanon, *Black Skin, White Masks,* trans. Charles L. Markmann (New York: Grove Press, 1967), p. 154.

3. Robert Coles, *Children of Crisis: A Study of Courage and Fear* (Boston: Little, Brown & Co., 1967). This book is a study of the effects of segregation on Southern black children.

4. Revelation 6:12–15.

5. James Baldwin, *The Fire Next Time* (New York: Dial Press, 1963).

6. Stokely Carmichael and Charles V. Hamilton, *Black Power: The Politics of Liberation in America* (New York: Random House, 1967), p. 35.

7. Philip Slater, *The Pursuit of Loneliness: American Culture at the Breaking Point* (Boston: Beacon Press, 1970), p. 26.

8. Paul Carter Harrison, *The Drama of Nommo* (New York: Grove Press, 1972), p. 33.

9. William E. Du Bois, *The Souls of Black Folk* (New York: Signet Books, 1969), p. 54.

10. Baldwin, *Fire Next Time,* p. 24.

It would seem to follow then as an indisputable fact that "we"—meaning by "we" a whole made up of body, brain and spirit, influenced by memory and tradition—must still differ in some essential respects from "you," whose body, brain and spirit have been so differently trained and are so differently influenced by memory and tradition. Though we see the same world, we see it through different eyes. Any help we can give you must be different from that you can give yourselves, and perhaps the value of that help may lie in the fact of that difference.*

—VIRGINIA WOOLF

4. Feminism and Straight White Males

Patricia R. Hill

CLIMBING THE FENCE

Over the fence—
Strawberries—grow—
Over the fence—
I could climb—if I tried, I know—
Berries are nice!

But—if I stained my Apron—
God would certainly scold!
Oh, dear,—I guess if He were a Boy—
He'd—climb—if He could!

—Emily Dickinson[1]

Emily Dickinson's gentle and subtle questioning of the social conventions governing female behavior—and of the adequacy of a male God image—contains all the essential reasons that compel me, as a woman and as a student of theology, to be a feminist.

40

The wistfulness, the sense of injustice conveyed by the delicate irony, the adventure (and the rewards) denied are all incorporated into a statement so complete that a woman can only respond with the affirmation, "Yes, that speaks to—and for—my condition!" To feminists in the twentieth century this quiet but powerful voice from the nineteenth is a reminder that we neither exist nor struggle in an historical vacuum, but that we can find strength and courage in our collective past. We can climb fences. We can reinterpret our theological heritage so that our struggle is affirmed and supported.

Emily Dickinson's poem—and its message—is even more amazing when the specific biographical context from which it emerged is examined. Outwardly she conformed—in all particulars except her refusal to join the church—to the expectations of a domineering father whose ideas were shaped by his strict and inflexible Calvinism. Her interior struggle was recorded in poetry which reflects a lifetime of searching done with an intensity of emotion and precision which both shocks and delights. The vast body of her work was written on odd scraps of paper and hidden in her bureau drawer only to be discovered after her death. That, in itself, is a telling comment on the limited sphere of expression allowed women in modern America. Dickinson's sister-in-law, recognizing the quality of her work, was responsible for preserving it. Not until well into this century did male critics finally take seriously the boldly creative and innovative use of language which distinguishes her poetry.

In not allowing herself to be bound by the conventional structures of language and of poetic models, Dickinson set a precedent which women today need to follow. She molded language to her own purposes, just as Jane Austen before her had rejected "a man's sentence" and had shaped a new sentence structure suited for a woman's use.[2] The language barrier is one that women need to climb if they are to use language rather than be defined by it.

Language is a subtle and complex force in and on our lives. So also is the socialization process which we all experience by simple virtue of the fact that we are social beings living in a defined culture. We know, without being entirely clear as to how and when we learned it, that little girls wear clean aprons, stay neat, and never go scrambling over fences. "Appropriate" role behavior is so engrained that it is reassuring indeed to hear Emily Dickinson protesting its limitations. To resist and reject traditional role models is a frightening thing to attempt alone. We need the support of our sisters in our struggle against a stultifying socialization process. Individually, we might be convinced that it is some defect in ourselves which makes us want to pick strawberries. Together, helping each other over the fence, we can begin to create our own roles.

My personal response to Emily Dickinson's poetry reminds me of a poignant graffiti exchange which I discovered on a restroom wall in Scotland. Someone had drawn with a purple felt-tip pen a simple sketch of a fetus sitting on a mushroom—an image which conveyed an unutterable sadness. Beneath it, in ball-point, another woman had written; "How could you possibly know?" Clearly, this reflected with a similar startled recognition an experience of communication on a level which cannot be defined by words alone.

I discovered in Dickinson's poetry the expression of thoughts and emotions which I shared, but which I had never imagined could be stated with such clarity, with such a sure and deft touch. Shared perceptions, the sudden realization of a common history—these are the source and power of the sisterhood which is central to the feminist movement. In the belief that what we have learned together as women about ourselves and our society can be shared with men as well as other women, and that it has implications for men as well as women, I address myself to brothers who are ready to hear a woman speak.

More specifically, I propose to explore three areas of concern to feminists which speak loudly to the condition of men trying to reinterpret their own lives and roles. The first is to reexamine history, looking for useful models and support from past radical analyses of culture. The second is to develop a more sophisticated understanding of language as a power which must be controlled if it is not to control people. The third is a conscious awareness of the socialization process, and the ways in which this awareness can help people break out of the prisons in which the process confines them.

RECOVERING HUMANNESS

The history of the systematic and pervasive oppression of women within the structures and institutions of Western culture has already been described and documented. Some of the nineteenth century feminists did a superb job of that in their explorations of the function of church and state in relationship to women throughout the Christian centuries. Contemporary historians have continued and expanded this work and have moved on to suggestive treatments of prehistory and the movement from matriarchal to patriarchal societies.[3] Feminists need no longer spend energy *proving* the fact of our oppression. However, an understanding of the historical roots and the growth of sexism provides a context and a perspective for considering its manifestations in contemporary culture. A radical philosophy of historiography which conceives of historians as "the critics of the culture rather than its apologists and perpetuators" has much to offer the feminist movement.[4] Continued exploration and documentation of oppression will serve to strengthen our criticisms.

Women do not need *proof* of oppression, but we do need to recognize the complexity and ambiguity of being the oppressed. This is especially necessary for those of us who are white, affluent, and educated; for we cannot allow our own oppression to shelter or excuse our participation in the oppression of others. Yet an awareness of ambiguity becomes dysfunctional if it prevents us from listening to and speaking out the truth of our collective past and our current experience. As critics of our culture, we must not neglect to criticize ourselves; but if our criticism is to be constructive, it must grow out of the refusal to continue silently to participate in our own oppression. Consequently, it *was* necessary to speak of and to document the history of the oppression of women as an integral feature of our culture. Now, our need for the strength and support of traditions and role models pushes us toward the recovery of lost history.

The silence maintained in conventional histories about women constitutes an implicit denial of the full and equal "humanness" of women. The tendency of male historians to subsume the experience of women under the category of generic "man" in writing the history of *human* civilization is indeed paradigmatic! Feminist historians are only now beginning to uncover the story of women which male historians failed to record. To reconstruct a past so largely ignored in the traditional "sources" requires a creative imagination and an innovative use of available materials. The feminist historian must look beyond formal records, letters, and diaries to myth, legend, folklore, and oral tradition. Archaeology and cultural anthropology offer evidence which ought to be integrated with the historical record.

The point, however, of doing feminist history and its real value

lies in the recovery of nonconventional role models and the reassurance that women did—and can—make valuable contributions
in fields traditionally considered "masculine." As that lost history reemerges from the past and merges into the social memory
of our civilization, the full humanness of women is affirmed.
Women can begin to see themselves—and hopefully men will
begin to see women—as creative agents, free to act and responsible for their actions. If the ability to climb fences is part of what
it means to be human, then the knowledge that women can and
have climbed fences forces the inclusion of women in the definition of humanness. Recovery of that knowledge, in and of itself,
becomes the record of a radical tradition.

The refusal to accept the dictates of cultural conditioning implies a radical questioning of basic cultural assumptions. If ours
is a culture in crisis, as has been suggested, then this radical
tradition offers a basis from which one can begin to challenge
current cultural assumptions. The ramifications of such a radical
reevaluation of culture involve men as well as women and operate
on a broader level than a specifically feminist agenda. Clearly,
this is a point on which feminism has much to say to those straight
white males who perceive the culture—as defined and per-
petuated by straight white males—crumbling, and current definitions of humanness too narrow for both sexes.

RECLAIMING LANGUAGE

Language is the medium through which we both name and
communicate our experience. The current emphasis on structural linguistics and the development of sophisticated linguistic
philosophy has revealed the extent to which the very structure of
the language we use shapes our perceptions and determines the
terms and categories in which we think. Through language,
either oral or written, we receive and transmit traditions. The
systematic analysis of and philosophical speculation on the function of language serves only to explain more completely to the
modern, scientific mind the power of language which has been
recognized and respected by both primitive and sophisticated cultures throughout history.

Indeed, in many cultures, the "naming" process, clearly connected to sacred ritual, is an important component of religious
practice. Among several American Indian groups, for instance,
individuals had names too sacred to be spoken except on the most
important ritual occasions. To speak someone's sacred name

was to exercise a very real power over that person. In other Indian groups, the naming process occurred as a part of the *rites de passage* from child to adult status and was usually derived from an induced dream vision. Undoubtedly, someone trained in cultural anthropology could fill a volume with similar examples from various cultures throughout the world.

Within the Judaic-Christian tradition one finds that Adam was given the right of naming all living creatures—including woman. The symbolic significance of this is such that it should come as no surprise to discover that the Judaic-Christian tradition has assigned a secondary and inferior role to women—and reinforced that role across the centuries!

Baptism is, of course, a sacrament in the Christian church, and, in most groups which practice infant baptism, has merged with the ceremonial christening of children. In the English-speaking world, first names are commonly referred to as Christian names.

The power of naming (understood more broadly than in the sense of proper names), lies in the fact that it limits and defines. In the context of this recognition of the power and effect of language, the insistence of feminists on "cleaning up" sexist language is validated. To argue that the generic use of "man" includes women and that masculine pronouns are used only by grammatical convention is to ignore the shock waves at the depth level of language impact. I do not feel "included," and I understand those pronouns to refer to me only insofar as I perceive myself an exception to, rather than a member of, my sex. What I hear being said is that I am somehow not a standard model of what it means to be human. The definition of humanness is expanded to include me only by the grace of grammatical convention.

Because the special power of language has so often been associated with the sacred, it is peculiarly fitting to examine the question of theological language from a feminist perspective. Theology as a discipline is predicated on the assumption that it is possible to use language to "talk" about God. Theologians, in their conscious efforts to use language with precision, demonstrate awareness of the connection between language formation and a sense of the sacred. In this, they follow the lead of the ancient Hebrews who, when referring to God in the synagogue, substituted the word "Adonai" for the name "Yahweh" because the latter was considered too sacred to be spoken.

Until recent years, theology has been a field not only dominated by men, but almost exclusively reserved to them. Not surprisingly, theological language, reflecting and reinforcing the patriarchal roots of the Judaic-Christian tradition, has assumed a particularly masculine tone. The pervasive use of male pronouns and imagery to conceptualize God, coupled with an assumption of maleness as characteristically human, makes the bulk of theological writing implicitly sexist. The interpretation placed on specific biblical passages (such as those drawn from the Genesis accounts of Creation and the Fall) compounds this sexism.

Christian theological models for femaleness have vacillated between extremes: Eve or Mary, temptress or virgin, whore or saint. True, in response to the feminist critique, an elaborate brief has been drawn up to prove that Christ was sexist in neither word nor action. Inevitably, in this context, some man points out that Christ defended Mary, the sister of Martha, against the criticism that she was neglecting her proper sphere. True enough. Yet fairness demands that the usual "use" of this episode be examined. In countless sermons this text has been distorted and twisted in praise of the Marthas of this world. Mary is virtually ignored because male clergy are uneasy with the implications of her role in the biblical account.

If women are not to be denied the power of language—and especially its power to invoke the sacred—then theological language and interpretations must be wrested from their present masculine orientation. If women are to invoke the power of language, we must begin to use it to name our own experience. We must reject a masculine definition of humanness. We must insist that if sexual imagery is to be used to suggest the sacred, it must no longer be exclusively male.

Emily Dickinson understood well the difference between being named and naming oneself. To her, the measure of maturity, the mark of full personhood, was the strength to assert her autonomy. The following poem, one of her most powerful, elaborates this theme in a specifically theological context.

> I'm ceded—I've stopped being Their's—
> The name They dropped upon my face
> With water, in the country church
> Is finished using, now,
> And They can put it with my Dolls,
> My childhood, and the string of spools,
> I've finished threading—too—

Baptized, before, without the choice,
But this time, consciously, of Grace—
Unto supremest name—
Called to my Full—The Crescent dropped—
Existence's whole Arc, filled up,
With one small Diadem.

My second Rank—too small the first—
Crowned—Crowning—on my Father's breast—
A half unconscious Queen—
But this time—Adequate—Erect,
With Will to choose, or to reject,
And I choose, just a Crown—[5]

Central to Dickinson's theme is the exercise of choice. Until we choose rather than accept our existence, and live out the affirmation of our choice, we remain children.

A conscious and continuing reappraisal of language involves a dynamic, creative dialectic between thinking and communicating. Because the exigencies of our situation as women in a male-dominated culture demand such a dialectic, feminists are creating patterns for approaching language as a powerful *tool*. These, if more generally applied to language use, might begin to reverse the tendency of our language to degenerate into cliché and jargon. Certainly, by clarifying the nuances, language can become more precise, and communication more effective. Reclaiming language to make it speak with precision and clarity is a task which will benefit men as well as women.

Putting Away the Dolls

A secondary theme in Dickinson's poem on baptism is the rejection of her childhood, the putting away of childish things. For the feminist, this must be a primary theme and a continual struggle. Dolls and strings of spools are symbolic of the socialization of little girls. To put them away, to be finished threading, is to move beyond the limits defined by socialization. Returning for a moment to the imagery of the poem quoted at the beginning of this chapter, rejection of socialization means no longer being frightened of a God who expects aprons to be kept clean—or at least ignoring that fear while you climb the fence.

Recognizing that socialization defines boundaries and shapes identity within prescribed limits will not free one from culture-bound patterns. Socialization is a process. Shaping forces do not stop molding simply because childhood and adolescence are behind.

The inculcation of cultural values and the process by which the internalization of role models is encouraged are, of course, more obvious in the preadult years. Fairy tales and television communicate "appropriate" sex role behavior to very small children; so also does the example and influence of parents and older siblings. Manufacturers of toys and clothing bring out products designed to encourage conventional sex role separation. Films and best-sellers portray conventional role models. The formal educational system utilizes textbooks which reflect sexist attitudes toward women and reinforce stereotypical behavior for both sexes. From research in educational psychology comes firm evidence that in the classroom expectations determine behavior. By logical extension, the same holds true within the cultural framework. It takes courage and continual effort to refuse to conform to socially acceptable patterns.

Expectations for culturally acceptable behavior—and responses which reinforce appropriate behavior—continue to function beyond adolescence. The complex forces of socialization operate more subtly on adults, but still effectively. Expectations are largely internalized. Failure to conform induces guilt and a sense of inadequacy.

For a woman, encouraged as she is in our culture to define her identity in terms of her relationship to a man—father, husband, or lover—the pressure to attach herself to a man becomes intense. Every novel she reads, every film she sees, and every television commercial she watches tells her that if she is a worthwhile person she will have a man. And she—God help her—believes the lie! Even the woman who has her "consciousness raised," who intellectually rejects the cultural conditioning to which she has been subjected, must continually confront the enemy within.

As socialization is a process, so also is the reverse operation. Women engaged in a radical questioning of their own socialization need the support of their sisters. Sharing the struggle generates a power which gives women the strength to confront culture. Individually, society could label each feminist a deviant—and alone we might begin to believe ourselves deviant. Together, we can challenge the definitions of deviance.

Males are, of course, also subject to a socialization process which rigidly defines appropriate behavior patterns for men. The ways in which socialization dehumanizes men as well as women are discussed elsewhere in this book. Only recently, however, have men begun to perceive current cultural models as restrictive and destructive—perhaps because in the past they have found conformity personally rewarding. Now, as men too begin to search, the models for reversing socialization being developed within the feminist movement speak to the condition of those men who want to escape their cultural conditioning.

"Doing Anything"

Helen Reddy, in her song "I Am Woman," articulated clearly the message that feminism has for straight white males: If we have to, we can "do anything."[6] We want to make our brothers understand, but if we have to, we can—and we will—continue on our own. We can no longer deny ourselves and sink again into patterns of submissiveness and dependency. We have grown strong in our struggle. We have learned much from each other. We have seen our culture through the eyes of sisterhood—and we are determined to change that culture. We have affirmed our humanity; and we will not again suffer ourselves to be objectified.

In sharing our collective past and supporting each other in our present, we have generated a power and an excitement which has the potential for radical cultural change. We invite the participation of our brothers in this process of change. We believe that men can share with women in a redefinition of humanness which can begin to challenge the forces of dehumanization in our society.

Straight white males who perceive their culture in crisis may find in a reexamination of history, a reclamation of language, and a reversal of socialization—according to feminist-developed models—the basis for a radical analysis of their own situation. Together, women and men can perhaps design new patterns of relating to each other—models based on the interdependency of the sexes. To do so would require the cooperation of men—*not* the capitulation of women. Feminists are determined to refuse dehumanization. We urge men to join with us in that refusal, but our decision has already been made. As sisters, we have helped each other climb the fence. That we had to do for ourselves. Now we are inviting men to pick strawberries with us. But we intend to eat strawberries in any case.

NOTES

*Virginia Woolf, *Three Guineas* (New York: Harcourt, Brace and World, 1966), p. 18. Copyright © 1966 by Leonard Woolf. Reprinted by permission of Harcourt Brace Jovanovitch.

1. Thomas H. Johnson, ed., *The Poems of Emily Dickinson* (Cambridge, Mass.: Belknap Press of Harvard University Press, 1955), 1:180–81. Copyright © 1951, 1955 by the President and Fellows of Harvard College. Reprinted by permission of the publishers and the Trustees of Amherst College.

2. Virginia Woolf, *A Room of One's Own*. (New York: Harcourt, Brace & World, 1957), pp. 79–80. Reprinted by permission of Harcourt Brace Jovanovitch.

3. See, for example, Elizabeth Gould Davis, *The First Sex* (New York: G. P. Putnam's Sons, 1971); Helen Diner, *Mothers and Amazons: The Feminine History of Culture* (Garden City: Anchor Press/Doubleday & Co., 1973); and Margaret Murray, *The Witch-Cult in Western Europe* (New York: Oxford University Press, 1962).

4. Howard Zinn, *The Politics of History* (Boston: Beacon Press, 1970), p. 13.

5. Johnson, *Poems of Emily Dickinson*, 2:389–90.

Homosexuals are sick. Very sick.

They're sick of wearing masks. They're sick of being snickered and sneered at. They're sick of being feared. They're sick of being called queers, faggots, and fairies. They're sick of being punished for being honest, of being labeled criminals by the letter of the law. They're sick of being barred from federal jobs and the armed forces. They're sick of being insulted on one hand, pitied on the other. Most of all, they're sick of being told they're sick.*

—HANS KNIGHT

5. Gay Liberation and Straight White Males

Charles R. Gaver

INTRODUCTION

In the fall of 1972 *Harper's* carried an article which "wished homosexuality off the face of the earth." The response from the gay community was swift and punitive. Gays organized a massive sit-in at the *Harper's* offices where a spokesperson, Peter Fisher, gave this warning: "What you don't understand is that there's been a revolution!" Fisher is correct on two counts. There has been a gay revolution. Gay people have begun to free themselves legally, psychically, socially, and politically. Their freedom has come partially from a rebellion against the prevailing heterosexual social norms. Gays have also, however, set about the task of creating *new* orders which bring with them new values, new directions, and new goals. Gay women and men are redefining themselves. They are radically changing their relationships and ties to present Western society.

But that is not the entire story. A second important point,

51

implied by Fisher, is that most people do not understand the gay revolt. They fail to recognize that revolution is a process, not an event, and that in the gay struggle the best has just begun. Blinded by traditional ignorance and contemporary prejudice, the American citizenry fails to see that when one enslaved group is combating oppression, those involved in the role of oppressor will not escape unscathed. What most people do not comprehend are the implications in gay liberation for their own lives.

This is particularly true of people who are defined by race as WHITE, by sex as MALE, by sexuality as STRAIGHT. The most privileged group in this nation, these straight white males are the people most likely, in the terms of Fisher, to misunderstand gay revolution. Why? Because they are raised to fear intra-sexual tenderness. They are taught to be disgusted by homosexual desire.

Sit-ins, like the one at *Harper's*, are meant to curb heterosexual bigotry, and to demand respect for this nation's sexual minorities. What I say here to straight white males is written with the vigorous hope that in a land where men are sanctioned to kill each other, they might instead begin to love one another.

NUMBERS: WHO IS HOMOSEXUAL?

At a recent gay workshop, this exchange took place between a participant and the lesbian group leader:

> "Supposing you're sixty/forty, or three-fourths and a quarter?"
> "Supposing you're *what?*"
> "You know, suppose you have just a tinge of homosexual in you."
> "Suppose you tell me who doesn't!"

The participant was puzzled. No names came to mind. The question has confused not only those in gay workshops, but researchers, geneticists, psychoanalysts, and others. Everyone wants to know: Just who is homosexual?

The famous Kinsey studies conducted during the late forties defined a "homosexual experience" as genital to genital contact resulting in orgasm. Kinsey concluded that 38.7% of all American men—forty million of them—had such an "experience"! These figures were shocking to the straight American public when published in 1948. They still have mind-opening impact today. But the importance of the Kinsey study to the gay movement lies not in its shock value, but in its blatant inadequacy.

Actions between gay people are not simply sexual. That is why studies which cite "practicing homosexuals" and quote figures like forty million are still of little value. The problem faced by the Gay movement concerns not "how many" but "who"! The first job of any cause is to define its constituency. In the case of the Gay Liberation movement, there is an obvious problem of identification.

Gays are not a visible minority in the same way blacks and women are. They are not "typed" by birth because of pigment or gender. There have been no identifiable constituents for the gay movement to draw upon, as there were in the other liberation struggles that preceded it. An endless number of descriptions have been attached to the term *gay*. One of the first was developed by the radical therapists in the mid-sixties. They claimed: "Gay is a state of mind." The corollary followed: "I think I am gay, therefore I am." Out of this mind-set came two groups: GAA (Gay Activist Alliance) and GLF (Gay Liberation Front). These were not psychiatric organizations. Their founders may not have been familiar with the Radical Therapist movement. Just the same, GAA and GLF began to elaborate on the RTs' "gay state of mind."

Unlike organizations such as the Mattachine Society and the Daughters of Bilitus which had existed for twenty to thirty years (and were secretive in membership and coy in political pressures), GAA admitted all who openly showed their support of gay freedom by attending a given number of meetings. Social programming took on strategic importance in a gay community that was becoming more and more visible. GAA sponsored everything from dances and picnics to writers' workshops and art shows in an effort to implement public awareness and solidarity.

What GAA did (and still does) was essential though not sufficient. GAA dances were sometimes disrupted. Artists who could get their works housed in gay galleries were sometimes discriminated against when they sought lodging for themselves and friends. Hence, GAA's political partner, GLF, came into prominence. GLF sought freedoms in areas that GAA had not dealt with explicitly. In the wake of this more militant organization, new definitions of what it meant to be *gay* soon surfaced.

GLF took a hard Marxist line. Gays were an oppressed economic class, branded by society as inferior and channeled into cheap-labor positions. GLF advocated the overturning of the present system of "corporate government" in the U.S. and carried its demands (for civil rights and against discrimination) to countless American city councils. But this was not the final re- defining of *gay*.

A third definition was quick to come via the Radicalesbian movement. Jill Johnston, a columnist for the *Village Voice*, launched the idea. Her argument is still being debated. No one can be a feminist, Johnston claimed, until she is a lesbian. The demand was for sexual separatism. After all, how could one be working for the women's cause when still sleeping with the enemy? Thus, meanings of the word *gay* expanded as rapidly as the movement itself. GAA spoke in terms of social participa- tion. GLF called for class consciousness. Radicalesbians saw *gay* as a political necessity.

All these definitions make sense. For those who are most famil- iar with gay politics, all these aspects of the term *gay* are often brought to mind. But what about one who has never paid GAA or GLF membership dues, nor read a word of Johnston's *Lesbian Nation?* A definition offered by the Homophile Union of Boston may help the reader understand why the word *gay* ought to con- cern him or her. HUB believes: "To be gay is to have the *capac- ity* for attraction to a person of the same sex, *and* to admit such an attraction when it occurs." Here, the essential aspect is that the concept is expanded from one focusing exclusively on genital contact to a view that allows gay relationships to flourish in emo- tional and intellectual areas, as well as sexual ones. One may well ask: Does that mean I'm gay? Does that mean everybody's gay? In a sense, the answer to both questions is yes. But there remains a *cultural* distinction that must be emphasized. Those who have suffered most from heterosexual repression are those who are most overt about admitting their homosexual attractions and acting upon them.

Owing to a Puritan heritage which decried sex outside of mar- riage, and to a Victorian moral code which decried sex *period* (except for procreative purposes), gays have been penalized most severely for their *sexual* preferences. Those who have been most honest and open about their sexuality have formed the core of what has come to be called the gay community. From this collection of up-front individuals have arisen new forms of life- style and alternative cultural values. These new values and ways of living are the contribution gays make to a nation now con- trolled by straight white males. It is the distinction between gay and straight norms and experiences that must be emphasized.

The aim is to advocate gay alternatives. The hope is that straight society will, for once, pay attention!

At the level of sexual activity, gays face habitual straight hostility. That must be emphasized! But that is not to minimize the difficulties of those who relate to the HUB definition in ways other than sexual. Imagine the plight of a young man who wishes to accompany a male friend to a dance. Not only would he face ostracism from parents and peers, but in many locations, legal ordinances forbid two members of the same sex from dancing together! This instance indicates the enormous extent to which straight cultural and legal codes harass gays. Has it always been this way? That's a good question. In order to comprehend how this nation became such a repressive state, one must look back a few thousand years. By examining the condition of gays in ancient times, one can discover the origins of contemporary forms of persecution.

Homosexuals in History

> Remembering
> What you, Christian, said:
> "When Jesus died;
> The Temple's Veil tore,
> Mystery no more, God's love
> Among us,
> Face to face,
> Beaming back."
> But add
> That it was only
> Man's face to woman's face, you meant
> Never woman's face to woman's face,
> Man's face to man's face
> Old hat tossed
> In a new ring.
> You'd drown us
> In hell fire—
> You and St. Paul—
> But our home is seaborne.
> Gay people
> Ride the Ark.[1]

From the beginning, there were gays. There always will be. Each successive society's treatment of homosexuals reflects its attempt or failure to deal with the fact that *indeed* "Gay people/ Ride the Ark." From the time of the ark, there have been many who branded gay love an "unnatural act." It was called "a crime against nature," though any good biologist knows that

homosexuality has existed just as consistently in the animal king-
dom as in the human one. But there is one difference. The
animals have yet to find a reason to wipe the gay members of their
species off the face of the earth. Several human cultures, however, have tried to do just that.

The original Reich of Western Culture (ancient Greece) made a
liberal allowance for male homosexual liaisons. Classic was the
case of a teacher-pupil relationship. The instructor or "elder"
(Socrates was a case in point) often slept with his male students.
Lesbians were not so lucky. Sappho, the famous gay Greek
poetess, had to resort to self-exile on an island called Lesbos
(from whence we have the term *lesbian*) before she could have
the same relationship with some members of her women's school.
At its inception, Western civilization *did* permit *limited* gay tolerance. "Tolerance" implies both "tolerators" and "tolerated."
That comes nowhere near the ideal of *acceptance* or *recognition*
of gays as legitimate people.

The Greek liberalism that produced such gay heroes as Socrates and Sappho collapsed into the hands of a more chauvinistic
Rome, and later turned to a completely intolerant "Christian"
church state. If gay people ever print up an "Enemies List,"
Paul will top it. Because he advanced such sick notions of
homosexuals as "whoremongers" and "menstealers," it is no
wonder that gay people are hated and feared throughout Christian
societies! We are just now beginning to see the reason why "the
early church *fathers*" felt homosexuality was such a societal
threat. Because gay relationships do not produce children, they
challenged the church's belief in sex for procreative purposes
only. A second reason why Paul and others were anti-gay is tied
to the Fall of the Roman Empire. Early church historians saw
the general decay and decadence of 2d and 3d century Rome; they
concluded it was caused by sexual freedom and feminism. Research today, however, has shown that the collapse of Rome had
little to do with the freedom of women or the tolerance of
homosexuality. Rather it was caused by a combination of
socioeconomic problems ranging from uncontrollable imperialism
to massive lead poisoning of the upper classes from lead-base
pottery. Even though we may question the church's dogma
today regarding acceptable sexual behavior, in "Mid-evil" times
many did not hesitate to carry out the Apostle's command:
"Who knowing the judgment of God, that they which commit
such things are worthy of death."

Such was the sentence pronounced on those engaged in homosexual acts. During the Middle Ages the letter of the law was carried out. It has been estimated that nine million women and gays were burned during medieval times. The word *faggot*, often used to insult gays today, was derived from the bundles of sticks that were used to kindle the stake fires:

When witches were burned in the middle ages,
the Inquisitors ordered the good burghers
    (all of them men, of course)
    to scour the jungles for jailed queers
    drag them out and tie them together in bundles,
    mix them in with bundles of wood
        at the feet of the woman,
        and set them on fire
        to kindle a flame
        foul enough for a witch to burn in

The sticks of wood in bundles like that
    were called faggots
and that's what they called the queers, too
and call us still,
meaning our extinction, our complete
    extermination,
androcide and gynocide their one response to
any heretical blasphemy against
a god-given manliness.[2]

From the first burning, the feminist and gay struggles were fused. The two movements share today, in addition to common members (lesbians), the demands for control of one's body, and legal guarantees of justice irrespective of gender.

From its Western inception, the persecution of gays and women, of "faggots" and "witches," led to a historical sense of common cause. This is not to say there is no sexism in the gay community. There is, just as there is anti-gay sentiment in conservative sects of the women's movement. But both causes have begun to eliminate prejudice and ignorance toward the other. Gay males understand that they have suffered in the same way as feminist women; neither conformed to the role assigned to their gender at birth. The cause for gay male support of the feminist movement is often not understood by the straight community; the reason may lie in the mix of ashes scattered in another age.

The beginnings of this nation meant only the makings of an American nightmare for gays. None of the groups that left Europe for liberty in the New World permitted sexual freedom.

When the U.S. Constitution was ratified, it supposedly guaranteed separation of church and state. But the religious biases against homosexuality are still incorporated in legal codes. The church has used the legal system to force its will on *all* U.S. citizens. Until recently, for example, pregnant women were not allowed to control even their own reproductive systems. The Supreme Court's ruling on abortion has indirect relevance for gays. It sets a precedent, suggesting that people can expect the Court to follow through and grant citizens sexual freedom in the same way it gave women procreative control.

Part of the reason court challenges have been so few is that there have always been places for gays to go when they faced hostility from straight neighbors. In early America, on the frontier, gay relationships flourished with convenience, if not freedom, among what we have come to call the cowboys.³ Ironically, if John Wayne were to portray a character from the Wild West with utmost accuracy, he might well be filmed having sex with his sidekick. The idea that the symbol of American machismo was sleeping around—as many cowboys did—is mind-jogging. Few people know about homosexuality on the frontier because prudish moviemakers have pumped up the cowboy mystique with legions of bonnet-clad "ladies." Actually, the women who did explore the frontier were usually those who refused to conform to feminine roles deemed acceptable by Eastern society. In addition to gay pioneers and cowhands the original settlers of the New World (native Americans–Indians) accepted homosexuality and transvestism in many of their tribes. But as the west was "tamed," so was the sexual freedom it permitted.

Activity among U.S. homosexuals, until the late sixties, was almost entirely covert. With the exceptions of Walt Whitman, Gertrude Stein, Alan Ginsberg, and James Baldwin, few Americans were public about any sexual or emotional preferences that were not heterosexual. Educators hid a subject's homosexuality: Whitman was referred to as the "good *gray* poet" all the time he intended to be known as the "good *gay* poet"! Students studied Plato's verse, never knowing that the names of young boys the love poems were written to had been changed to names of female gender. The same is true for Shakespeare's homosexual sonnets!

Homosexuals hid away in the final American frontier, the city. Along with blacks, Jews, and immigrants, those with "foreign" sexual preferences sought the freedom of anonymity accorded residents of large urban areas. For the longest time gays were underground. Then, in the summer of 1969, something happened in New York City which brought gay people and gay issues instantly and violently to the surface once again.

Judy Garland had been dead one week. Some of her followers, most of them gay, had been mourning her demise in a Manhattan bar, the Stonewall Inn. It was June, 1969. Early one evening the police began a routine raid. This time, however, something very unroutine occurred during the vice squad's harassment. As one participant remarked: "For once we faggots fought back!" Led by the transvestites, transsexuals, angered street queens, and lesbians, the brave gays picked up bottles and bricks and battled the cops until reinforcements came. The streets have yet to be emptied!

The insurrection at the Stonewall Inn is commemorated every year in "Christopher Street/Gay Pride" parades. Avenues everywhere from New York to San Francisco are filled with thousands of marchers. Organizations such as GAA and GLF have marched into city councils and courtrooms, racking up legal victories. Laws have been changed or challenged, though in all too few areas. But some of the accomplishments include removal of sodomy as an offense from the codes of Hawaii, Illinois, Connecticut, Ohio, and Oregon, as well as guarantees of full civil rights and an end to discrimination in housing and employment in the District of Columbia, Ann Arbor, and San Francisco. Detroit, East Lansing, Minneapolis, Seattle, and Berkeley have amended several laws. Some church and psychiatric organizations (along with the Civil Service Commission and the American Bar Association) have reversed long-standing anti-gay positions and are calling for full civil rights for homosexuals. Meanwhile, the militance continues.

Every time gays were harassed in the "merry-go-round" area of Philadelphia during the summer of 1973, fire alarms were pulled. Mayor Rizzo's administration finally decided it would be cheaper to end vice-squad action than to fuel fire trucks after every false alarm. Politicians have tried to ignore the Gay/Human Rights Bill on the books in Ann Arbor. They have subsequently found their city council meetings disrupted. Hundreds of publications, television studios, and radio stations have been picketed and *zapped* (a term that includes anything from sit-ins to impromptu demonstrations in front of TV cameras). It is a wonder most zaps have been nonviolent, for after centuries of being burned and beaten, one might expect gays to advocate all-out war!

Slowly, with uneven but deliberate efforts, gays have begun to fight back. In the face of hundreds of years of historical repression, attempted genocide, and humiliating discrimination, the Stonewall riots have signaled the birth of gay resistance and, ultimately, liberation! Gays are making gains. The question then becomes: What does this mean for the class of people on whom gays are gaining?

GAY GOALS AND ALTERNATIVES

> my mind is ©
> do not discover what
> i have discovered without consent
> in writing. someday you will
> listen to your own voices
> & poets will be irrelevant
> i am not the keeper of the faith[4]

It has been the intention of the straight white male state to divide and conquer gay people: to isolate them, to make them feel inadequate and inferior, and then to encourage self-mutilation and destruction. As the above poem suggests, gays, like every oppressed group, must begin to control their own communities, *to listen to their own voices,* to determine their own lives. "WE WILL DEFINE OURSELVES!" as Stokely Carmichael has demanded in the context of the black struggle. So far, this self-determination has not taken place, especially in American media. As a friend remarked: "How many hermaphrodites have you seen on the Doris Day Show lately? And never have I tuned in to *Jeopardy* to find them competing for an 'Answers' category of 'Famous Faggots for $10'!"

One wonders if gays haven't been somewhat fortunate in escaping this sort of treatment. Nevertheless, the lack of positive gay identity models has hurt. The straight white male image-makers have devised a "Model American." One is either the "wife" or "husband" of a nuclear family which produces 2.2 children and enough U.S. savings bonds for a duplex in White Plains and Easter vacation in Jamaica. Those who differ from this ideal are punished economically and ignored socially. Above all (especially in the case of gays who rarely carry with them symbols visible to other members of their oppressed group) those who are "different" are stung with the terrifying fear that they are *alone.*

For this reason, steps have been taken to combat gay isolation. Witness the birth (about 1968) of gay communities: entire geographical areas in which homosexual residents predominate. Examples range from Manhattan's West Village to an entire county in Colorado. What some have chosen to call "gay ghettos" in center city Philadelphia, Georgetown, D.C., and Boston's Beacon Hill, as well as large chunks of Portland, Los Angeles, Atlanta, San Francisco, Seattle, Detroit, Chicago, and even Cleveland, have supported and produced businesses, churches, health centers, community entertainment, and educational programs. Most important for gay people themselves has been the sense of *belonging* that had formerly been lacking.

The original gay activists can take credit for much of this regrouping. They required a confessional statement of gay faith that made it easier to recognize who chose to belong and who chose otherwise. It is called "coming out." The process has to do with first reconciling one's homosexuality to oneself; and secondly, going public with the knowledge. Being "out" refers to being free from the *closet* (a term applied to those who hide their homosexuality). "Coming out" is a trying test, but it has formed a much-needed common bond between gays. And it did something else; it freed people. As gay activist Arthur Bell has written: "There is nothing as protective as blatancy. When you've nothing to hide, there's nothing to protect."[5] By thousands, gays of all ages have stopped hiding, have become "blatant rather than latent," have begun to be accepted for what they really are, not for what heterosexual chauvinists would have them *pretend* to be.

Each time another individual comes out, it has relevance for exclusively-straight society. Lifestyles that gays have forged, in spite of heterosexual hostility, are at last coming of age. Gay *activism* has become gay *advocacy*. Homosexual communities have fostered the support for major changes in heterosexual culture as well. As Huey Newton of the Black Panther party maintained: "There's nothing to say that a homosexual cannot also be a revolutionary. Quite the contrary, maybe a homosexual could be the most revolutionary." If Newton is right, he will be proven so on specific issues which pit the more egalitarian aims of gay liberationists against those hypocritical and oppressive institutions sanctioned by straight society. One such area for debate concerns the very nomenclature itself. The question becomes: What's in a name?

The term *straight* refers to a bland, bigoted manner of existing, as in the phrase *straight and narrow*. Part of the problem with un-gay people is just that: they are too inhibited to enjoy and celebrate the gay things in life. The "gay ghetto" is one of the most creative places in America. Though sometimes the site of economic deprivation, homosexual communities often feature one of the most festive atmospheres in any city. Houses are brightly decorated both inside and out. During the warmer months, the streets and sidewalks are streaming with people.

There are dances sponsored by community groups, "paint-ins" encouraged by next-door neighbors, parades, picnics, or poetry readings like those held periodically in Philadelphia's gay bookstore, *Giovanni's Room*. There is danger in creating a romantic stereotype. Not all gay communities are chummy and cheery. Some are the endless scene of police harassment and aggression from bigoted straights. But highlighting the "gayest" aspects of gay ghettos is done to explain that, given a little breathing space, homosexual residents are trying to fashion enjoyable, friendly, and fun places to live.

There are also quite a few homosexuals who are still "closeted" in all-straight suburbs, acting out the fantasy of being the only flannel-jacketed fairy in the country club. Just as blacks are co-opted into a white world and become "oreos," so has the gay community produced its own breed of "Auntie Toms." The solution is not one of absolute separation. Indeed, many straights continue to live happily in gay ghettos. But the closet case who laughs at faggot jokes and votes against gay legislation (all the time sneaking into gay bars for a quick pickup every weekend) is not doing either community any good, and ought to be banished by both. Those who are above board about their behavior should be rewarded and respected for their honesty. Until certain changes are made by the larger heterosexual establishment, gays must continue to support and nourish alternative communities and values.

One place change must occur in the straight society is in the area of *sex*. Gay people are not obsessed with putting "things" in "holes." Homosexuality is not only genital to genital contact. Gays have developed a sexuality that treats the entire being as an erogenous zone. Straight sex has too often degenerated into a mechanical process—genitally-centered, orgasmically-oriented. Heterosexual books are crammed full of position after position, a myriad of acrobatic stunts, all a variation of the same "thing-hole'' concept. Part of the straight problem with sex dates from the church's emphasis on the procreative act. Since gays have never been hung up with reproduction, they have been freer to enjoy sex as an end in itself.

At last we can approach sex, not as a utilitarian function (a means by which to ''breed'') but as both an affirmation of self and a sharing with another in a pleasurable act. Imagine! No more ego trips over who is on top, literally or otherwise. Rather than erogenous zones being the sources of combat and exploitation, sex might finally be appreciated for the pleasure, not the offspring it produces. Perhaps some day, straights will take a lesson from gays. Sex of all types will begin to develop into more *whole* ways of *loving*. The gay precedent has already been established.

In addition to *sex* as a subject viewed differently by gays and straights, there is the issue of *sexism*. Jill Johnston is explicit when she calls for the making of a ''lesbian nation.'' She advocates the complete separation of gay-feminists from straight-sexists. The former would maintain a matriarchal state in which private property and male supremacy could be abolished. The author is explicit about male aid in achieving feminist goals:

> The oppression of women is pivotal in the strategy and goals of the gay sexual revolution. The more overt discrimination and persecution of the male homosexual makes this point clear. I mean that the hatred of the gay male is rooted in the fear of the loss of male power and prestige. Since society accords many special benefits to men it is considered worse for a man to ''act like a woman'' than the reverse. The upfront gay male surrenders his prestige in a sense by acknowledging he is not participating in the system by oppressing the woman where her oppression begins—in bed.[6]

There are still too many gay men who are either not ''up-front'' about their homosexuality or share sexist sentiments held by a large number of straight males. Johnston's statement provides insight into what gay ways of living can do to challenge heterosexual sexist norms. Tasks are not performed in gay relationships on the basis of sex. They could not be. If two men are living together, one may do more housework than the other, but the role is not one determined by gender.

Most gay partnerships tend to ignore the traditional traps of someone playing ''wife'' and the other playing ''husband.'' To try to emulate the very culture that has degraded gays would be masochistic; thus gays have opted for more egalitarian models.

Straight couples in need of unsexist images might find many available in gay communities. Marriage, for instance, has become quite constraining to certain heterosexuals. Gays have been living together without that institution for centuries, and their comments about how to survive in a hostile social climate are just what many straights need to hear.

Finally, with regard to the subject of sexism, those who do not agree with Johnston's gay-separatist attitude must still admit that homosexuality can break down barriers that cause women to fear and envy other women, and keep men competing against and destroying other men. Rather than the heterosexual tyranny of the *Playboy* philosophy, where males dominate and females sublimate, homosexual encounters can mean a more positive view of one's self and one's sex. Ms. Johnston explains:

> It's my decree. To be a woman was wrong. To be woman who loves woman double wrong. To be woman who loves woman and says so was unthinkable. It was in the same words unthinkable to love yourself. To say so now is the revolution.[7]

Through gay love, women have become less alienated from each other and themselves. The same is true for many gay men. Those who have criticized homosexuality as narcissistic fail to heed the warnings of an ancient teacher: no one can love others until they love themselves.

It is one thing to love oneself. It is another to be so self-indulgent and self-righteous that you cannot laugh at your own foolishness and arrogance. Such is the lesson of a major gay cultural contribution, that of "camp." Some of camp is sexist, but a large part of it is neither bigoted nor self-denigrating. Until recently, few straights knew much about it. As Bruce Rodgers says in his dictionary definition:

> camp. (slang) 1. One of the most famous and used of all homosexual slang words, *camp* became celebrated linguistically in 1968, when pop culture discovered the word: overnight everybody knew what it meant. Only they really didn't.[8]

Pop culture was not the only group confused about camp. Susan Sontag wrote a widely read essay on the subject in the *Partisan Review,* and critics tested the term against everything from the works of Andy Warhol to Gloria Vanderbilt's wardrobe.

To define *camp,* one first has to identify with it. That is the greatest of difficulties. *Camp* is to gays as *soul* is to blacks as *kitsch* is to Jews. It is a social outlook unique to one's culture. In camp's case this includes a reverence for once fashionable clothes, words, or ideas which are no longer in style in the larger society. It is the worship of forgotten movie stars, gaudy hats, or "loud" interior designs considered by straights to be "in bad taste." It is the preservation of manners and material objects that straight society has tossed out, as it has homosexuals.

Not all campy objects or notions are to be found in heterosexuals' trash cans. More often, camp is an attitude of mocking what straights idolize: framing pictures of Dick Tracy, papering a bathroom wall with shopping bags from Saks Fifth Avenue, hanging Christmas ornaments in July. Those who cultivate camp seem to be saying: "I identify with the fashions and manners heterosexual society has turned its back on, because in a similar sense, and for no better reason, I have been rejected too." In the same vein, camp artists seek to ridicule the most sacred of straight customs. What has evolved is a gay guerilla warfare with quite mind-opening tactics:

> I never understood the camp fascination with the movies of the thirties and forties until the Cockettes (a transvestite theatre troupe) finally brought home to me just what was happening. Movies and movie stars aren't trivial or peripheral to American culture. They teach people what it means to be a man or a woman and how you should act as one or another—"Love American Style." A man is like John Wayne, a woman is like Lana Turner. . . . If one of the basic tyrannies of this society is the roles men and women are forced into, then the popular culture of movie stars and starlets, western heroes and popular romances enforces this tyranny. They teach people they must be brawling insensitive clods to be real men, passive simpering ornaments to be real women.[9]

Theatre troupes like the Cockettes in Mike Silverstein's "God Save the Queen" are part of the reason straights need to look closer at camp. By performing selections from straight plays and films, groups like the Cockettes demonstrate the sham and hypocrisy of sexist roles. Gays, however, are in no way immune to self-criticism, and many a camp crack has been directed against homosexual hypocrisy as well.

Heterosexual humor has too often been *only* at the expense of other racial and ethnic groups rather than being useful in illustrating the foolishness within straight society itself. A campy outlook has permitted gays the freedom to never take themselves so seriously that they'd seek to commit mass murder against those

who differ from their outlook. Indeed, straights have a great deal
to learn; that is, presuming everything they need to know can be
taught.

WHERE WILL IT LEAD US FROM HERE?

Perhaps a mind that is purely masculine cannot create, any-
more than a mind that is purely feminine.[10]

—Virginia Woolf

The emphasis on developing a truly bisexual populace is, I
believe, the most valid goal of gay liberation. People ought to be
free to enjoy the best of both sexes, as well as to seek a better
balance between the masculine and feminine in each of us. But a
bisexual society is a long way off for important reasons, the major
one being the straight white male. This class of people has an
economic as well as an *ego*centric stake in oppressing gays and
blacks and women. Straight white males have legislated and
enforced laws which discriminate against homosexuality.
Through the church, the schools, and the media they have taught
that gay people are sinful and dangerous and neurotic. Until all
forms of sexuality are held as being equally valid and healthy,
bisexuals must join with gays to fight oppression of their
homosexual attraction.

To accomplish this will take decades of unlearning the prejudices that straight white males have whipped gays with since the
beginning of Western civilization. Churches must cease being
used as a chauvinist weapon against those who engage in sex for
other than procreative reasons. As suffragist Elizabeth Cady
Stanton suggested over one hundred years ago, the Bible will
have to be reedited. Passages that reinforce the oppression of
women and gays must be revised, reinterpreted, or eliminated
altogether. Gay historical and literary contributions cannot be
ignored by academics. Curricula will have to add gay studies
alongside courses on black heritage and feminism. As for the
mass media, gay rock stars have already come of age in the image
of David Bowie and others. But the battle for equal time has not
even begun. A Washington, D.C. television station has produced a regular five minute news-spot called "Shades of Gay,"
which attempts to enlighten viewers on homosexual culture in the
nation's capital. But for every "Shades of Gay" shown on D.C.
television there are a dozen "hairdresser" jokes aired on radio
stations and repeated in publications all over the country. Gays

seldom attain even the "token" status black actors in films and theatre are just beginning to get beyond.

In the area of economic discrimination those gays who have been fired or denied promotion because they were honest must be monetarily compensated. Blacks in the late sixties demanded reparations for indignities pinned on their ancestors. Gays must speak for the same, so those who fought before them will not have suffered for nothing.

When no more antagonism is incurred by those who choose any sexuality other than a purely "hetero" one, when burnings and chastisings of gays cease, when straight society purges itself of sexist practices and sexual chauvinism, then a truly whole sexual humanness can be proudly cultivated. As far away as that may seem, some gays have already begun to pursue the need for a more open view in their communities. Some call it "bisexual potential." Laura Della Rose, in an article for *The Gay Alternative*, said:

> Implicit in my use of the term 'Bisexuality' is my feeling for, and experience of the inevitability, joy, and beauty of gayness. But another assumption emerges—both sexes have to come to terms with each other physically and sexually, not just verbally and politically, for the honest caring and good faith that is a basis for workable and cooperative coalitions. Sexual attraction is just one aspect of human relationships, but it's a damn motivating one.[11]

Ms. Della Rose views bisexuality as a mode of communication between gays and straights. She points out that not only must the two cultures reconcile their political and social differences, but the physical barriers between the two must be broken.

Another gay who agrees is Phil Mullen who writes:

> The truth is that the entire human body, male and female, is a potential source of sexual pleasure for everyone. Only a bisexual ideal will make us aware of that possibility.
> Now that we're finally learning that gay is good, we'll have to start learning that gay isn't good enough. Some of us, obviously, will be able to make more progress in this area than others.[12]

These two writers echo the ideals espoused by many of today's gay activists who call for a society where choices of any kind (from job opportunities to sex) are not made on the basis of gender. This ideal is a completely androgynous one. Human beings will develop and pursue both masculine and feminine traits and behaviors, and will be regarded by one another as *people,* rather than "men" and "women." Both heterosexual and homosexual choices then will be of equal value and respect.

As Mullen concluded, some will make more progress in this area than others. Some already have. Straight white males will probably be the last to achieve their bisexual potential, because they have the greatest stake in the heterosexual cultural setup that brings them economic, social, and sexual benefits to the detriment of everybody else.

Unfortunately, it is often easier for gays to advocate bisexuality today because they can only gain in the eyes of a society where straight sex is still the seldom contested norm. Too many Americans see bisexuals as heterosexuals who play around on the side. For this reason, heterosexuality, even as practiced through the chic pretense of "bisexuality" *can* be a destructive guise. For women, heterosexuality means giving vital energies to the oppressor. For men it means draining revolutionary energies from the oppressed. For gays bisexuality can be a cop-out, by one's allegiance to the (hetero-) sexual institutions that presume themselves superior to homosexual ones. This, none of the above can now afford!

If women are to be free, they must give each other support (and that means sexually too). If men are to be liberated, they must give each other love (again, in *all* forms). If gays are to become viable in American society, they must affirm their own lifestyle before they can participate in others that are *already socially acceptable*. The case of the bisexual who tries to minimize homosexual attractions while being "public" about heterosexual ones, is not unlike the Jew who hides his or her religion, the black who shuns the company of other blacks, or the Puerto Rican who seeks to speak English with no trace of a Latin accent. All are forms of self-denial. Straight white men, and their institutions which encourage "closet" Jews or gays or Third-World "oreos" and "coconuts," are doing themselves more damage than they realize. Straight white men who demand that members of alternative cultures become imitations of themselves will succeed in getting *more* people to support the *same* cultural forms that brought us everything from Indian reservations to imperialist ventures like Vietnam.

One asks: Would *anyone*, who had a choice, buy a used (and defective) culture like the bigoted, inhibited one being advertised by straight white males? Many gays, having realized that they *do* have a choice, want no part of the "majority" view. But too often it is unprofitable and sometimes suicidal to live in open opposition all the time. For homosexuals who must give up their freedom for reasons of employment, for example, it has been suggested that they ought to share the profits of their secrecy with gays who are trying hard not to hide. Anonymous contributions (not often enough!) are made by conscientious but closeted homosexuals to gay newspapers, health centers, hot-lines, bookstores, and civil rights organizations. There is something potentially revolutionary (and certainly satisfying) about homosexuals who scrape together a few extra dollars from big-oted straight employers, and send them to gay rights organizations to help fight against such prejudice.

It is people like the "Auntie Toms" or flannel-jacket fairies participating in the pickup syndrome who further oppression of gays. The reason gay people turn to handouts and prostitution is that they are denied employment by straights. Those closet cases who cruise the streets of gay ghettos trying to exchange money, food, or a place to sleep for sex, may well be helping their "trick" to survive, only to repeat his or her prostitution. If so-called providers were really sincere about the survival of their gay brothers and sisters, they would contribute even more effort and cash to organizations involved in equal employment opportunity suits on behalf of homosexuals. Then gay sex would cease being exploitive in such cases. As in any oppressed group, some of our greatest enemies are those who have internalized the bigotries of the oppressor, and are among us. But the *worst* enemy is still the straight white male, whose ancestors devised this oppressive system and who today *continues* to benefit from it.

I believe that eventually we must reach a state where our society, our friends, and our "families" can respect us as *sexual beings*—regardless of the gender(s) of our partners. But until all forms of sexual expression are considered equally valid, bisexuals must ally themselves with those forms which are not. A bisexual who will not work for the cause of gay liberation is a hypocrite. Society has no qualms about heterosexual activities of bisexuals, while it seeks to minimize, repress, and devalue their gay capacities.

Until gays have secured their basic rights and due respect, "bisexual potential" will remain impotent. In such a sense, the revolution that Peter Fisher referred to at the *Harper's* sit-in has yet to be completed. Straights must revolt against their narrow cultural values, as gays continue to challenge heterosexual norms from without.   Together the two cultures can free themselves by freeing each other.   For, in the end, we will be one, or we will be nothing at all.   Gays have been doing more than their share to fight sexual and sexist repression.   It is time that effort was reciprocated.   So goes the message to the straight white male: I'll lend you a hand when you're able to take mine!

NOTES

The Sunday Bulletin (Philadelphia), 19 July 1970.

1. Linda Marucci, "Untitled," *The Gay Alternative*, 6 (1974):27.

2. *Flaming Faggots Collective* (Ann Arbor, Mich, 1920).

3. Myron Brenton, *The American Male* (Greenwich, Conn.: Fawcett Publications, 1966), p. 31.

4. *Burn This and Memorize Yourself* (Washington, N.J.: Times Change Press, 1971).   Copyright © 1971 by Alta.   Reprinted by permission of Times Change Press, Penwell Road, Washington, N.J.

5. Arthur Bell, "Gay Is Sweeping the Country," *The Village Voice* (April 4, 1974), p. 25.

6. Jill Johnston, *Lesbian Nation* (New York: Simon & Schuster, 1973), p. 183.

7. Jill Johnston, "Ave Atque Vale, Guillaume in Pax," *The Village Voice* (November 4, 1971).

8. Bruce Rodgers, *The Queens' Vernacular: A Gay Lexicon* (San Francisco: Straight Arrow Books, 1972), p. 40.

9. Mike Silverstein, "God Save the Queen," *Gay Sunshine* (November, 1970).

10. Virginia Woolf, *Three Guineas* (New York: Harcourt, Brace & World, 1966).   Copyright © 1966 by Leonard Woolf.   Reprinted by permission of Harcourt Brace Jovanovitch.

11. Laura Della Rose, "Bisexual Potential," *The Gay Alternative*, 6 (1974):22.

12. Phil Mullen, "Sexual Reform or Revolution," *The Gay Alternative*, 6 (1974):14.

Part Three

From the Masters:
To Themselves

The alienated oppressor must learn what it means to be truly responsible for whom and what he is.*

—ROSEMARY R. RUETHER

6. The Oppressor Dehumanized

Glenn R. Bucher

Liberation, as we have seen, begins amidst despair and hope. It grows as a new bud out of the ashes of oppression. Straight white males can be hopeful about their eventual freedom when they are ready to examine the despair which they have caused others. We have heard a black man, a white woman, and a male homosexual speak of their continuing struggle for freedom amidst forces that insist on continuing enslavement. Their statements confirm the ways in which the life stories of straight white males intersect with those of blacks, women, and homosexuals. They also establish the framework within which liberation for straight white males can be discussed. But before that happens, one prior task stands out: those who are white and male and straight must talk to themselves about their dehumanization as the oppressor, and about their whiteness, maleness, and heterosexual preference. The present chapter is devoted to a consideration of oppressorhood and dehumanization.

THE STATUS QUO

In ordinary times, the status quo is worth no one's attention. Why speak of what is? How can anything be special about normalcy, about business as usual, about everyday routine? Rather, is it not the future about which concern must be expressed? About the present, nothing more can be done. At least these seem to be popular responses to the situations in which many live, and toward which they look.

72

But these are not ordinary times. The normal is abnormal. It preoccupies those who view it from the bottom up. The oppressed contend that the status quo is corrupt, that business as usual cannot continue. Life's givens are not neutral. Rather, the times are laden with values so distorted that to speak of the present as prelude to the future is to doom the future. It is important, therefore, to speak of normalcy in America because straight white males are high priests of the status quo. They continue to sanctify it religiously. It *is* what they *are!*

Oppressed groups only confirm our "Confessions" in chapter 2 that American normalcy is racist, sexist, and straight. The tragedy lies not only in the way *social marginales* are oppressed by the abnormally normal, but also in what has happened to those straight white males who perpetuate this oppression. To be the functionaries of a social arrangement which dehumanizes is to be dehumanized oneself.

About the values intrinsic to the status quo, there may be ignorance or disagreement. About what is normal there can be no doubt. Examples are legion. If the oppressed's charges are legitimate, then the everyday life of a straight white male will verify them. Straight white males need look only to their daily lives for illustrations of oppression and dehumanization.

The American symbol of normalcy embodies a wealth of circumstantial evidence: a middle-class straight white male; married and a family man; a good citizen who loves money, wife, children, and flag. Little more needs be said; almost any television commercial features him. You know of whom I speak. What is obscure—because obvious—is that in the aforementioned description there are powerful statements about the economic, social, and legal realities that surround us, those everyday realities which necessitate the oppressed, presuppose the oppressor, and create the dehumanized.

The economic reality is best seen in an economic condition known as middle-classness. Most straight white males in America are middle-class and enjoy it. Jobs and lifestyles are linked directly to it. But do we ever think about how the middle class came to be, about the injustices on which it relies, and about the repercussions of both for blacks, women, and homosexuals?

The economic reality has been particularly burdensome for black Americans. The American system of slavery arose primarily for socioeconomic, not racial, reasons. As the worldwide demand for tobacco and cotton increased, America's labor requirements grew. For those straight white males standing to profit from the economic upswing, the question of cheap labor arose. Blacks were chosen. They were strong, inexpensive, visible, unprotected by political arrangements, and inexhaustible in number. Economic desire motivated the enslavement of black people. Without cheap labor, our economy would not have developed as it did. Slavery assured that part of the backbone of the American economy would be black Americans.

That was then. What about now? Consider the judgment of Robert L. Allen:

> Black people cannot afford the social injustices of capitalism. They cannot afford a system which creates privileged classes within an already superexploited and underprivileged community. They cannot afford a system which organizes community resources and then distributes the resulting wealth in a hierarchial fashion, with those who need least getting most. Neither can black people afford some half-hearted compromise which would make the black community in general, and its educated class in particular, subservient to the expansionist needs of corporate capitalism.[1]

If American-style capitalism was slavery initiated, then contemporary social injustices, privileged classes, and capitalistic expansionism are only natural, predictable by-products. An economic system built upon injustice cannot become just without major overhaul. Such an overhaul has not happened in America. Consequently, those who enjoy middle-classness are implicated in the history and present realities of that status.

Whether it be median income, unemployment, or poverty, blacks always come out on the disadvantaged end. For white families, median income has always been substantially higher than for black families. Among blacks, the unemployment percentage is always higher. And considerably more black than white youth grow up in and are subjected to the conditions of poverty. What can one conclude from all of this finally, except that the American economic system is racist? One significant group, black Americans, has been among its victims from the start and, essentially, remains where it always was. Relatively few blacks have escaped the group predicament. It is this economic system which, by word and deed, most straight white males in America affirm daily as they pursue their vocation and enjoy its benefits.

The economic dinosaur, unfortunately, is not the only monster which inhabits the middle-class zoo of straight white males. There is also a social reality, a way of life having qualities of a warm puppy: marriage, home, and family. It is that center around which most straight white males mold their lives. Few modes attract more attention, concern, sentiment, and compassion than the American home. How could anyone intimate that this institution shares anything in common with the economic inequalities just described?

Many straight white males do not know that marriage and family are under attack today. Women of the liberation movement are exposing the sacred estate. The 1963 publication of Betty Friedan's *The Feminine Mystique* is notable: it marked the beginning of the contemporary feminist movement popularly known as Women's Liberation.[2] Friedan declared that middle-class American women are tired of household drudgery—for which she had some colorful terminology. "Radical" feminists claim that marriage equals slavery; that freedom of women will be secure only when marriage as an institution is abolished.

Unfortunately for those who think otherwise, there are legal supports for this view. According to American law, marital responsibilities of the wife revolve around the performance of domestic chores—cleaning, cooking, washing—necessary for stable home maintenance. In addition, she is to care for husband and children. On the other hand, the legal responsibilities of a husband are to provide a home for his wife and children and to support, protect, and maintain them. For the husband, the duty is to maintain essential structural security, whereas for the wife, marriage constitutes the contract whereby she is charged with home management. This inequality of status is accented further if one examines the legalities associated with marital sex. In marriage sex is compulsory by law. A husband can legally force his wife to have sex against her will. In the marketplace, that is considered rape! For the married male, sex is a right; for the female, a duty.

Other abnormalities about this normal American institution are also apparent. The marriage-home-family syndrome is designed to serve the male species. It provides security in love, sanctuary for children, and services for the husband. It is the wife who manages the daily details of this estate. She rears the children, cooks the meals, cleans the house, washes the clothes, and does the shopping. In short the woman *manages* the home. Some would insist that the home is her natural habitat. What is important to note is that all these homemaking services by women are provided for men. Men, consequently, are freed to address themselves to a vocational agenda, which usually includes the pursuit of success, wealth, social prominence, and self-satisfaction.

There are, no doubt, serious objections to this description. Surprisingly perhaps, many in the women's movement would reject its moderation out of hand. What is even more disturbing for any straight white male participating in the marriage-home-family nexus is to analyze critically his modus operandi. Most males relate to their established home as we have described. Essentially, the American home is a gasoline station/motel for straight white males. To it they come for a renewal of energy (food, sleep, sex, and human exchanges). From it they go to expend energy in behalf of professional goals. This syndrome above all others is considered "normal" in American society. As in the case of the economic system vis-à-vis blacks, however, so with the marriage-home-family institute: it necessitates the oppressed (wife), presupposes the oppressor (husband), and creates the dehumanized (the family).

Finally, the legal system which straight white males maintain and from which they profit must be mentioned. We seldom give thought to this legal reality, the institution which undergirds and structures the life of our society. We do not entertain, ordinarily, the possibility that the law itself violates human beings. Because something is legal we usually assume it must be just. For homosexuals in America, however, that is not the case.

American laws controlling sexual behavior vary from state to state. But copulation between husband and wife is the only sexual act that is nowhere a crime. In one state or another, other forms of marital loveplay, solitary masturbation, premarital or adulterous sexual behavior are all crimes. Usually only the antihomosexual applications are enforced, either by the police or by public opinion.

Given the moral substructure which undergirds law and the public consensus which provides for its interpretation and enforcement, it is no surprise that homosexual offenses are severely punished. Almost all states render some or all homosexual acts a criminal offense, even when carried out by consenting adults in private. The maximum penalty for these felonious "crimes against nature" ranges from ten years to life imprisonment. Most states have statutes covering homosexual misdemeanors which carry lesser punishments. Almost any sexual gesture or act is punishable under these statutes.

Oppression in America comes in various shapes and varieties. Paralleling the legal abuse of homosexuals is the public sentiment at work to determine behavior in the common sector. Male sex organs are associated with strength and social roles; males are therefore socialized to be predatory, aggressive, competitive, and calculatingly reckless. At the emotional level, they are discouraged from displaying tenderness, compassion, affection, or sentimentality. In our society crying and open displays of emotion are forbidden. With feelings bottled up, the male is expected to establish a career, be a "gentleman," marry, and raise a family.

The male homosexual symbolizes rebellion against these social expectations. "Homo," "faggot," "queer," and "freak" are the dominant culture's response to this rebellion. Social reinforcement of heterosexual preference continually operates against those males who choose otherwise, and the legal system adequately reflects public consensus. Homosexuals are perceived to have violated, in addition to the law, the norms of society. That offense is the most serious of all. Society has developed elaborate mechanisms for handling such criminals.

Thus the normal, everyday life of a typical straight white male intersects with the economy, the home, and the legal system, and in status quo America these realities are not devoid of human values. In addition to serving legitimate functions, they are also oppressive systems—for blacks who continue to be economically enslaved, for women who do not enjoy equal social status in the home they maintain, and for homosexuals who suffer at the hands of an unjust legal system. All this is integral to normal American life. That is what many straight white males fail to grasp. The status quo is racist, chauvinist, and sexist. It necessitates the oppressed, presupposes the oppressor, and creates the dehumanized. As straight white males profit from normalcy in America, they are implicated directly in its oppression.

TO BE THE OPPRESSOR

The oppressors are identified. Although it is unlikely, some straight white males might ask: "What can we do to help those suffering from oppressive injustice?" Though partially valid, we do not want to entertain that query. It assumes that the oppressed need straight white male help to correct the aberrations of an otherwise just social order. We have argued that the social order is not just; it is intrinsically oppressive. To go to the heart of the matter of liberation is to address the oppressor and not the oppressed. Hence, the only question for us now is: "What can straight white males do for themselves?" That is a new question. It is a radical one because it goes to the root of psychosocial oppression in America. It presupposes that straight white males need liberation from their role as oppressor and from their dehumanization.

In an important book about the oppressed *(Pedagogy of the Oppressed)*, the Brazilian philosopher Paulo Freire says:

> The oppressor is solidarily with the oppressed only when he stops regarding the oppressed as an abstract category and sees them as persons who have been unjustly dealt with, deprived of their voice, cheated in the sale of their labor: when he stops making pious, sentimental, and individualistic gestures.[3]

Freire claims the oppressed "have been unjustly dealt with." That has foundation in fact, as we have already seen. It is not only the oppressed, however, who constitute a social category, but also those who are their oppressors.

Sociologically speaking, to be the oppressor is to be the social norm and reference point against which every definition of abnormality is judged. Whiteness, maleness, and heterosexuality are presumed to be the human criteria against which all others are measured. This is clear in sociological discussions of "deviancy." In 1942, C. Wright Mills, a renegade sociologist of that period and the years since, described normality as understood by his colleagues (the "social pathologists," as he labeled them):

> The ideally adjusted man is "socialized." This term seems to operate ethically as the opposite of "selfish"; it implies that the adjusted man conforms to middle-class morality and motives and "participates" in the gradual progress of respectable institutions. If he is not a "joiner," he certainly gets around and into many community organizations. If he is socialized, the individual thinks of others and is kindly toward them. He does not brood or mope about but is somewhat extrovert, eagerly participating in his community's institutions. His mother and father were not divorced, nor was his home ever broken. He is "successful"—at least in a modest way—since he is ambitious, but he does not speculate about matters too far above his means: lest he become "a fantasy thinker," and the little men don't scramble after the big money. The less abstract the traits and fulfilled "needs" of the "adjusted man" are, the more they gravitate toward the norms of independent middle-class persons verbally living out Protestant ideals in the small towns of America.[4]

Mills describes a social norm which straight white males still embody. Against this model all other social creatures are evaluated. Those who are not middle-class; who do not participate in respectable social institutions; who are not products of a "stable" home; who cannot claim they are "independent middle-class persons verbally living out Protestant ideals in the small towns of America," are destined to be social exceptions.

To be the oppressor, then, means to be the human social norm. It is to have social prejudice, society's mores, and public morality tilted in one's direction. It is not to worry about respectability or respect. It is to be comfortable. It is to be familiar with social expectations. It could not be otherwise, given that straight white males also determine both the social rules and the punishments for those who fail to conform. For straight white males American society is a warm, wet womb wherein environmental conditions are very congenial.

Already we have said that economic realities point to a racist system. To the extent that this system discriminates against women and homosexuals as well as blacks, none save straight white males are spared the agony of being "cheated in the sale of their labor." Predictably, the median income for families with male heads far surpasses that for families headed by women. Likewise, women—on the average—earn considerably less than men. "Equal pay for equal work," one of the demands of the women's movement, is modest in light of these realities.

But what of the economic dimensions of oppressorhood? To be the oppressor is to exploit labor and profit from it. Whether we speak of blacks in cotton fields (or their contemporary equivalents), women qua mothers in the home whose labor is free, or homosexuals discriminated against vocationally due to sexual preference, the conclusion is verifiable: straight white males perpetuate these economic arrangements, if in no other way, by their tacit approval of the economic benefits thereby procured for themselves. To be the oppressor is to be master of the "American plantation." A glance at the constituency of any corporate board, or the roster of America's chief corporate administrative officers, puts to rest any doubt.

There is another dimension to these economic conditions. Unfortunately, males have derived their identities from, and defined themselves in connection with, "having" and "doing." To be is to have and to do. Both having and doing involve economic activity. To have pertains to possessions; to do suggests vocation. But straight white males have made certain that both vocational status and the accompanying economic rewards which make possessions possible are partially denied to those they oppress. In this sense, then, to be oppressor, economically speaking, is to enforce, condone, and exploit a double standard. It is to say to the oppressed that their humanity does not deserve or require the economic rights which whiteness and maleness and heterosexuality demand and assure.

To be the oppressor in the economic arena is also to be committed to charity amidst injustice. Freire calls it "false generosity." This "sensitivity" manifests itself in such things as fruitbaskets at Christmas, welfare checks, bonuses, and overtime pay. By supporting these "doles," straight white males recognize economic injustice and, therefore, need. But they seldom propose something other than modest gratuities in order to redeem the imbalance. As Freire understands from his Third World perspective as a Brazilian philosopher, false charity is integral to economic oppression. It gives those who perpetrate injustice something gracious to do, while perpetuating that economic arrangement which makes necessary this form of charity. To be the oppressor, then, is to indulge oneself in meaningless giving.

The oppressed "are deprived of their voice." That is a political statement. Watergate, a symbol of our time, is important for us here because, with only a single exception, those who played leading roles in the Watergate comedy were *straight white males.* (One can only speculate about the possibility of Watergates in a government *womanned* by blacks, females, and homosexuals.) This single example indicates that political power in American society is in the undisputed hands of straight white males. All we need do to speak, politically, of the oppressor is to mention Watergate.

To be the oppressor is to *control* the political process at the expense of others. To be in control of events and processes is a need engrained in most straight white males. It insures domination. Politics provides the arena in which the control is exercised. For example, in the 1972 presidential election 41 million males, 45 million females, 78 million whites, and 7 million blacks voted. All these figures are proportionally consistent with general population statistics. Yet the Ninety-third Congress included only 13 women in the House and none in the Senate, 15 blacks in the House and one in the Senate. Add to this the Watergate statistics and our contention is validated: straight white males exclusively control the governmental processes despite the fact that there are 104 million females in the country as compared with 98 million males. Whiteness and maleness and heterosexuality assure political control.

To be the oppressor is to absolutize one's political behavior and to insure that it remains above legal reproach. Fines and sentences tend to be inversely proportional to the whiteness and maleness of those found guilty. The final legal disposition of Spiro Agnew symbolizes the preferential justice of which we speak. Few other citizens, particularly blacks, would have enjoyed his judicial success: the fines he paid are incidental compared with the 40-year jail term he might have received. The Watergate conspirators too have benefited from their privileged status. The entire legal system is dominated by straight white males. Those who contend that American justice is consistent are correct: It insures absolution for almost any straight white male political behavior.

To be the oppressor, then, is to participate in the phenomenon of oppressorhood. Through a curious mixture of decision and default, straight white males in America *are* what they *do*. Being and doing are inherited, as well as acquired. Straight white male oppressors—much like those they oppress—are not necessarily self-made persons; they are social products over which, initially, the persons themselves have little control. By the time some semblance of consciousness develops, the straight white male versions of being and doing already are ingrained. That is, straight white males are oppressors, irrespective of what they *want* to be. Oppressorhood has reality. To be the oppressor is to categorize impersonally the oppressed, to be the dealers and not the dealt with, to be the deprivers and not the deprived, to be the cheaters and not the cheated. No human being can exist in such a circumstance and not be adversely affected by it. Hence, the oppressors are also dehumanized.

To Be the Dehumanized

The oppressor has been identified. Straight white male roles determine their being. They too are "oppressed," though we shall reserve that word primarily for blacks, women, homosexuals, and others whose oppressions have led to historically obvious suffering. To refer to straight white males as *dehumanized* expresses the tragedy of which we now must speak. As Freire says, "dehumanization which marks not only those whose humanity has been stolen, but also (though in a different way) those who have stolen it, is a *distortion* of the vocation of becoming more fully human."[5]

The oppressor's dehumanizations assume various forms. As a consequence of participating in the economic, social, and legal oppressions described earlier, straight white males distort their potential for humanness. Economically, the oppressor is dehumanized because the maintenance of oppression is expensive, produces less than human results, and is not in the total self-interest of even the oppressor. High taxes necessitated by police protection, welfare payments, and social services for the poor are the direct result of racism and sexism. Without perpetual injustice in the economic arena, the protection of property, the subsidization of income, and public services for those unable to pay would be unnecessary. Essentially, these expenditures are required only so long as the oppressed exist. And the oppressed exist only so long as the oppressors want them to. Dehumanization is not limited to the useless expenditure of funds, and the indirect toll it demands from human life. But so long as a sizable portion of income is taken by the state in order to support the continuous oppression from which he benefits, the straight white male remains economically dehumanized. Economics separates human beings from one another on a permanent basis. And economics designed to reinforce and perpetrate an already unjust economic arrangement is doubly inhuman.

The politics that produced Watergate has dehumanized all Americans. The "nation with the soul of a church" has been exposed as soul-less. There is tension in the society, within the individual spirit. Americans seem adrift in a sea of confusion and despair. The political consequences of Watergate are not purely political; they are also moral and spiritual. Among the young people selecting vocations for life disillusionment is rampant and disgust enormous, and all because the straight white males of Washington were carried away by their normalcy, by their ambition, courage, and pride—all of which are the normal hallmarks of "health." To suggest that Watergate has in spirit dehumanized a host of young men, potential lawyers, politicians, and public servants, is to understate the case.

Straight white males are dehumanized in very personal ways as well. Why do hypertension, heart attack, stroke, ulcers, and nervous breakdowns occur so frequently among us? Statistics are not necessary to establish causality. These maladies are directly linked to what being a straight white male in America has meant, means, and continues to demand. It is not humanly possible to live up to the expectations we have set for ourselves in terms of achievement and success. Yet we insist on trying. The result is predictable. Even more tragic than the pressure syndrome itself is the fact that physicians and researchers have approached these medical problems in pursuit of symptomatic cures. The treatment for heart disease is sophisticated, the comprehension of its emotional wellsprings comparatively, primitive. Straight white male physicians are caught in the same trap as those they seek to help. Obviously the oppressor is victimized by social expectations which have medical consequences.

There is an emotional parallel to this. Straight white males are dehumanized because they are emotionally deprived—deprived in the literal sense because they are allowed few expressable emotions. One is expected to show his fellow males little or no tenderness, compassion, affection, or sentimentality aside from a warm handshake or a slap on the back. And public crying or other displays of emotion are viewed with disdain. Clearly, the straight white male is socialized into an emotional robot; to be a whole human being, he is taught, means negatively speaking, *not* to be emotionally immature. Emotional expression is not possible for males who aspire to the prevailing American image.

Evidence of psychological dehumanization is also abundant. Alienation from self is, by definition, dehumanizing. Yet this is the condition of many straight white males. Because the society is dominated by us, we feel at home in it. Most straight white males uncritically accept the model set forth for them by the society. They are social products par excellence. But this leads to self-alienation. We do not know who we are, apart from that which others have told us to be. Any individuality latent in our being is repressed. The consequence is alienation from one's uniqueness, one's needs, one's emotions. Simply because straight white males do not acknowledge this alienation is no reason to believe it does not exist. Many are unknowingly dehumanized. But we are no less dehumanized for our unknowingness.

Being the oppressor thus has human consequences of many sorts for those who play that role. One's finances are affected because oppression is expensive. Economics insures the alienation of human beings from one another; that is not in the self-interest, ultimately, of those perpetuating oppression. Oppression has moral and spiritual consequences, as well as personal ones. And the emotional and psychological price paid by straight white males is high. Essentially, self-alienation is the result, and that is antithetical to human wholeness.

That straight white males are the oppressors is not only the contention of blacks, women, and homosexuals. It is also the conclusion one is forced to reach in an examination of straight white male normalcy. By virtue of their status, straight white males function as oppressors vis-à-vis the oppressed, but the result is dehumanization for themselves. It is one thing to hear that from others, and another to discover it for ourselves. The discovery is both frightening and exhilarating: frightening because one is confronted with who he is, and exhilarating because liberation begins with insight and with movement from one circumstance to another.

NOTES

*Rosemary R. Ruether, *Liberation Theology* (New York: Paulist, 1972), p. 16.

1. Robert L. Allen, *Black Awakening in Capitalist America* (Garden City: Doubleday & Co., 1969), p. 274.

2. Betty Friedan, *The Feminine Mystique* (New York: Norton, 1963).

3. Paulo Freire, *Pedagogy of the Oppressed* (New York: Herder & Herder, 1970), pp. 34–35.

4. Quoted in Herbert Aptheker, *The World of C. Wright Mills* (New York: Marzani & Munsell, 1960), p. 72.

5. Freire, *Pedagogy*, p. 28.

Come now, you rich, weep and howl for the miseries that are coming upon you. Your riches have rotted and your garments are moth-eaten. Your gold and silver have rusted, and their rust will be evidence against you and will eat your flesh like fire. You have laid up treasure for the last days. Behold, the wages of the laborers who mowed your fields, which you kept back by fraud, cry out; and the cries of the harvesters have reached the ears of the Lord of hosts. You have lived on the earth in luxury and in pleasure; you have fattened your hearts in a day of slaughter.

—James 5:1–5

7. The Meaning of Whiteness

Patricia N. Dutcher

Confronting Ourselves

White Americans are being angrily confronted by the oppressed and poor everywhere. In our own country there have been sit-ins, demonstrations, protests, and lawsuits aimed at whites and white-run institutions by blacks, latinos, and native Americans. Worldwide, we have come under fire from peoples of assorted political leanings in anti-American demonstrations, riots, kidnappings, and threats to American corporations. Our most cherished and highly regarded institutions (schools, courts, the military, foreign aid, business, the Central Intelligence Agency) and some of our favorite myths about our way of life—its charity, honesty, beneficence—have been attacked and degraded by those who characterize us as oppressive, imperialistic, and exploitive.

White Americans have attempted to defend themselves. We have rebuked the challengers and reiterated the high qualities of justice, peace, and opportunity that we uphold in this country and throughout the world. But the answers of white Americans, on the whole, have a hollow ring. To even the most reasoned and articulate questioners and challengers we have issued defensive reactions, not thoughtful reassessments. In a time when "most Americans operate on the unarticulated theory that if everyone gave just a little more to Community Chest and if all businesses hired just one more black man, the American (racial) crisis would be solved,"[1] the accusations of oppression and exploitation appear groundless and discriminatory. Many white Americans, refusing to believe that there could be any truth to the criticisms, defend themselves in a naïve and unquestioning manner.

But there are a growing number of whites who feel that we must not cut off discussion with a mindless denial of the challenges. As the evidence accumulates that the things white Americans say and do are oppressive, we must do more than merely issue denials; we must take seriously the charges of oppression and examine ourselves. In previous chapters we have heard how blacks, women, and gays specifically challenge the straight white male. Also we have heard about the dehumanization of oppression. In this chapter we shall look more closely at whiteness from the inside and inquire about its meaning. Here we shall deal with it not simply as a racial notion. Whiteness will be examined in terms of the social, political, and economic ramifications of the ideals and lifestyles of whites and of the institutions and culture of white society in America. Defining whiteness this broadly, we can consider those patterns in our lives which work to oppress others. We will look especially at two facets of oppression, paternalism and exploitation. We must locate their sources in white society and their consequences for oppressed peoples at home and throughout the world.

Understanding our oppressive patterns requires that we look at ourselves critically and clearly. To do so will necessitate using harsh language, terms with which most Americans are not used to being described. But we must not shy away from delineating the patterns of oppression which, unless described in clear and unequivocal ways, can easily be overlooked in our generally uncritical view. This is what Knowles and Prewitt had in mind when they said about racism:

> America is and has long been a racist nation because it has and has long had a racist policy. This policy can be understood only when we are willing to take a hard look at the continuing and irrefutable racist consequences of the major institutions of American life.[2]

While being descriptive we do not want to be too judgmental. It is not necessary to find evil causes or pernicious motivations behind our actions. The oppressive actions described are not those of consciously evil and oppressive people. We are not looking for villains, but for roots of oppression within ourselves and for the correlations that exist between being a white and being an oppressor. In sum, we want to describe the oppressive results of the institutions and society in which we live and from which we benefit.

PATTERN OF OPPRESSION: PATERNALISM

Most white Americans concede that we have a race problem in the United States. Despite our best efforts to help blacks and other minorities, they still suffer from countless "deficiencies." Many are poor, uneducated, unskilled. Some are even worse off—prone to crime, undisciplined, lazy. From our perspective the race problem seems essentially a problem of the blacks (and latinos and native Americans) themselves. They need help, jobs, skills, education. Minorities, we feel, are likely to cause trouble, commit crimes, be on welfare and disturb the peace and order of our society. We have nothing against blacks as people. But black communities in our cities and towns are socially "sick." They often have high crime rates along with excessive and rowdy behavior; they are dirty and unkempt, a breeding ground for lawlessness and social problems. We believe that black communities need our help to survive and tight police control to keep peace. Most importantly, we know that the solution to the race problem lies in teaching blacks to do things the way they should be done. Though highly questionable, these are the prevalent views of white America.

By contrast white America, it seems, has much of which to be proud. We know the importance of law and order, neat and clean communities, hard work and perseverance. Our system, based on freedom, justice, democracy, and equality, has produced one of the best societies on earth. We have quite a stock of virtues including rationality, a command of scientific and technical knowledge, a competitive spirit, education, a striving for peace and order. And, most of all, we are successful. What we work for, we accomplish. What we fight for, we win. Again, the popularity of these attitudes does not guarantee their legitimacy.

As we look from our healthy white society towards the unhealthy black and minority communities, we find roots of oppression in the attitude that characterizes the relationship between white and black groups: paternalism. Whites feel we can or must control the behavior of blacks because they cannot take care of themselves. We must paternalistically regulate their conduct, set limits for them, supply their needs, and teach them skills. Through the historic idea of a "white man's burden," we feel the need to shoulder the responsibility for the poor, blacks, and other minorities. In some instances, many whites have felt that it is our religious or moral duty to help them. We have succeeded in creating a healthy, vibrant society. Why should we not teach others our way of life? After all, if everyone could live like us, they would be better off. Such is the view of many a white liberal.

The charity of whites may be sincere, but the net effect is racist and oppressive. Implicit in it—in fact at its very heart—is the assumption that whites are good and superior, and minorities are inferior and must become like whites. The processes used are numerous—blacks educated in white-run schools, blacks given no options but to comply with white-designed programs, blacks taking on white-designated roles, blacks meeting white criteria for success. The end result is the same: blacks are to become like whites and fit into white society. The key element in this paternalism is not that the blacks have decided to become like whites, but that the whites have decided that for them. Blacks must deny not only their heritage and people, but also the basic human right and need of self-determination.

Our paternalistic attempts to make "inferiors" better by making them "white" is not confined to our shores. Over the course of the past century we have extended our influence and our white burden to include the poor colored masses of most of the rest of the world. The aid and charity extended by Americans for health, education, and social facilities in poor countries have in fact bettered the lives of many people. But we should not be startled if our self-congratulations are cut short by angry criticisms from Third World people who resent the paternalism inherent in our aid programs. Along with our sincerest wishes comes the assumption that the poor colored masses, their countries and cultures, are inherently inferior. Because they are inferior, we feel that they not only need our aid; they also need to learn to do things as we do them; to think as Americans, and to accept whatever parts of American culture we regard as best for them. This Americanization process has destroyed elements of native institutions and cultures which ultimately would have been better suited to changing the lives of the poor; in their place it has substituted the unachievable goal of becoming like affluent white Americans.

Many white Americans are oblivious to how our paternalistic racism belittles and degrades other races. We participate unknowingly in oppression, the goal of which is to make others become like us—for their own good! While the forms and programs of our aid have changed over the years, the paternalism in them has remained constant. Yet the white American, even the most liberal among us, never notices his paternalism.

> Even now, when he has learned to talk about "giving people options" to choose between styles of life, it rarely occurs to him that they might in the end prefer something other than what he imagines for them, or that they could resent his efforts to help them out.[3]

PATTERN OF OPPRESSION: EXPLOITATION

If white Americans were only paternalistic towards Third World peoples, then we might escape criticism by reforming our more obnoxious practices. But the oppressive nature of white society does not end there. Not only in the attempts to convert others to the "white is right" way of life, but also in the daily workings of our system, we are oppressive. While we have tried to define the problems of the poor and oppressed as *their* problems, we have refused to see that *we* are the problem. We ourselves are largely responsible for the conditions that oppress. Blame cannot be placed elsewhere. Oppression is not the fault of the oppressed themselves.

We must recognize that our lifestyle, our culture, our institutions require in their normal operations the perpetuation of exploitable and exploited groups both at home and abroad. It is we who create and maintain oppression. The domestic situation can be characterized in this way, even though the "realization" is applicable worldwide:

> A new realization is dawning in white America. Under the insistent prodding of articulate blacks plus a few unusual whites, the so-called "Negro problem" is being redefined. Just possibly the racial sickness in our society is not, as we have so long assumed, rooted in the black and presumably "pathological" subculture, but in the white and presumably "healthy" dominant culture.[4]

Realizing the truth about our exploitation will be more painful than facing up to the fact of our paternalism. It is not easy to accept the demythification of our good self-image, as Knowles and Prewitt point out:

> The false assumption, that the poverty of the ghettos is best attacked directly through the war on poverty, welfare, and the countless other ghetto-oriented programs, has caused white people to overlook the more basic issue of racist attitudes and institutions that shut black people off from the instruments of self-determination. A problem cannot be solved unless it is attacked at its roots, but when the roots are found entwined in the lives, communities, and occupations of white people, it is far easier to place the blame elsewhere than to face up to their own responsibility.[5]

There is an element of contradiction between the two patterns of paternalism and exploitation: our sincere but paternalistic goodwill hopes to make everyone as well-off as ourselves, but our desires for profit, power, and influence contradict that goal to the extent that they require the continued existence of exploitable groups. This contradiction is more apparent than real. In practice it actually works to our advantage. We have convinced ourselves—and have tried to convince the oppressed—that our actions are only for their good. In this way we can disguise and ignore the exploitative nature of our relations with oppressed peoples, both domestically and internationally. However, it must be noted that we have done a much better job of fooling ourselves than of fooling the oppressed. We have even reached the point of believing that our exploitive actions are actually good for them.

The irrefutable evidence of our exploitation of others emerges as we look at ourselves and our history. The blatant examples of oppression exist: of blacks under slavery and Jim Crow; of immigrant workers under inhuman working conditions; of native Americans from our push west into lands of the "savages." In each case, the pattern is the same. Economic, social, and political exploitation of other races and those of lower social standing is perpetrated by and for the benefit of a relatively few rich white people. All this is done during what the few consider to be "the normal course of events": at the time we did not consider the killing of Indians, enslaving of Negroes, and overworking of immigrants as extraordinary—these occurrences were part and parcel of the accepted American way of doing things.

Again today the patterns of exploitation show up, still not obvious to whites but no less a part of the normal course of events. Blacks and Puerto Ricans are forced by white housing codes to live in ghettos where white landlords and merchants seek profits from the poor. Migrant workers are forced into laboring in the fields for long hours, unprotected by the laws that protect white workers. Native Americans' last remaining and sacred land and water are destroyed by the ravages of stripmining in the West. Latinos are pushed into slums and deprived of civil rights because of *their* language problem.

Exploitation occurs at many levels and via many institutions. Where income, housing, health care, quality of education, food, and legal advice are concerned, blacks, latinos, and native Americans always end up with less so that whites can have more. Some battles have been won in the long, uphill struggle, and some superficial changes in national priorities made during the more socially-conscious late sixties. But the exploitive situation is still a part of white society. Whites are still on top. Especially in less affluent times, whites always emerge with the best jobs, houses, and social amenities.

The plain fact is that exploitation exists and we as whites are its beneficiaries. Money goes into our pockets; resources feed our industries; power and privilege are retained by our institutions. And, as ever, this still seems to us to be "nothing out of the ordinary." Even if we do not recognize it, however, exploitation is in fact a normal part of the way we do things. Because the status quo works to our advantage, there is no reason to question it. But because we never question it, we never realize the exploitation that is inherent in it. Who would question the profit motive, long so determinative—and "beneficial"—in the individuals?

> The condition of the black man in America reveals that whites consider their pocketbooks to be far more important than their morality. The failure to respond to gross historical exploitation seems to give final support to those critics of capitalism who see it as an economic system which denigrates man and encourages exploitation.[6]

As with paternalism, exploitation extends well beyond the borders of our own country. In a world where most of the established American institutions are no longer national but multinational, our oppression affects many of the euphemistically-termed "developing" countries. They may well be developing. But they are more accurately described as "poor." And the system most adept at taking advantage of that poverty is lodged in the U.S.A. The evidence is fast accumulating that "man has indeed amassed the power he has sought, but at the expense . . . of the large majority of humanity which has been exploited in the pursuit of power by the few."[7]   Obviously, it was not we who made the poor nations of the world poor. But we have willingly fed ourselves off their continuing poverty and have exploited the world's powerless masses to our own gain. We are thus accountable for the perpetuation of a significant part of the poverty which plagues the Third World today.

The exploitation experienced by many of the world's people is a result of several aspects of the interlocking American multinational institutions. Again, we need not look for villains, or evil people deliberately bent on oppressing others. We need only see the several factors of prime importance in maintaining our power in the world: the need for dependable sources of raw materials to sustain our industrial growth nationally and internationally, the need to maintain a foreign trade balance advantageous to the United States, military security of the United States and of its interests around the world, profitability of American investments in other countries, and in general the maintenance of United States influence and power in world affairs. These factors, and the institutions pursuing them, add up to a comprehensive and integrated system of U.S. owned, operated, and controlled power bases around the world. The collective normal everyday operations of these institutions effectively exploit much of the population of the Third World. The forms of exploitation may not be as readily recognizable as those of the old-style colonialism which we all now disavow, but the effects are fully as real and oppressive.

Just as whites domestically strive to maintain their control of the principal societal institutions, so white Americans, through our government, strive for political control in world affairs. While we may share the power with others (Europeans and other elites), we feel it to be an utmost necessity that we influence or control much of what happens in other regions, ostensibly for the good of others but principally for our own security and prosperity. The pursuit of peace and aid for the poor are honorable and worthwhile goals. But the protocol politics of American foreign policy can also work to oppress. In the East-West power plays, Third World countries are often relegated to the role of "satellites" of us good guys who support democracy and oppose communism. We still regard it as important that none of our "friends" be lost to the "other side." The effect of such a policy, however, is to reduce poor nations to pawns who take orders from and remain under the influence of our diplomatic and military might.

Our worldwide military network gives the appearance of providing security. But it also proves handy in suppressing any Third World liberation movements that are considered to be too radical and, by our standards, communistic. In the pursuit of freedom and democracy, Americans have supported, aided, and even created authoritarian, military, oppressive, and dictatorial regimes in Third World countries. Indirectly through these governments, and directly through such actions as giving military assistance for suppressing political radicals and guerrilla movements, Americans participate in the oppression felt by many of the poor countries.

At the forefront of the American institutions that perpetuate injustice are the multinational corporations, a group of business interests that includes many of the largest and most powerful industrial and financial corporations of the United States. While many of their foreign investments are in Europe, and while the Europeans themselves own many large multinationals, it is crucial for white Americans to be aware of the international control and influence of these companies, in which many of us own stock. Their influence in the Third World is extensive, pervasive, and oppressive—and "necessary":

> What matters to the business community and the business system as a whole is that the option of foreign investment (and foreign trade) should remain available. Maintaining the open door creates problems, some because of conflicting interests among the more mature capitalist nations, some because of the actual and potential social revolutions which threaten to eliminate (or limit) capitalism and freedom for private investment and trade. Hence, opening the door and keeping it open require eternal vigilance and willpower. What is needed, in other words, is the strength and persistence on the part of the more advanced nations to influence and control the politics and economics of the less advanced nations.[8]

Third World countries serve as sources of two items of major importance to corporations: profits and raw materials. On the profit front, investments (and trade) provide opportunities for inexpensive labor, tax breaks, and numerous special concessions needed by developing governments hungry for industrialization. The sales potential, markets for short and long term credit, and work forces of Third World countries provide good business con-

ditions for American investments—good unless disrupted by social unrest, or radical group attacks on foreign business interests,
or unfriendly governments. All of these negative factors can be
discouraged, however, by the oppressive working of other
American interests ranging from foreign policy considerations to
foreign aid payments, from overt military involvement to covert
military and Central Intelligence Agency operations.

Through financial flexibility provided by the transnational web
of investments in subsidiaries and affiliates, corporate profit rates
can be further increased by transferring goods, taxes, and profits
among countries to maintain the highest possible consolidated
profit for the American parent company. Because multinational
companies transcend the political boundaries and regulatory
powers of all governments, let alone the weak governments in
poor countries, they can operate without the political accountabil-
ity that their size and power would otherwise dictate. Many
development-minded governments have been reluctant to do anything to discourage investments by these multinational grants;
they even give the companies special concessions and latitude not
accorded their own national companies. Thus the multinational
corporations frequently enjoy both a freedom to seek their goals
of profit and control, and an insulation from negative political and
economic considerations.

Although there are always some problems, generally their goals
are met: overseas investments are almost always the most profit-
able branches of American business. It has been shown that,
despite the supposed "investment" of capital in underdeveloped
countries the multinational corporations actually take more resources *out* than they put in. This spells simple exploitation, in
which by way of loans and profits businesses from rich countries
milk the economic resources of poor countries. They maintain
the control that is all important for international corporations. In
some countries, American companies own or control significant
proportions of the economy and monopolize entire industries.

Profit and control are available by way of other arrangements
as well. By controlling and licensing technology, multinational
corporations determine the availability of important resources ur-
gently needed by developing countries. Similarly, such technological licensing arrangements allow American companies restrictive control of both the domestic and export markets of their
developing-country competitors. They thereby damage the
financial viability and growth possibility of the poor countries'

few industries. When the profit, credit, and technological advantages of American multinational corporations are combined, the economies of Third World countries are often reduced to secondary roles in providing for their people. The oppressed become wholly or largely dependent upon the foreign companies, companies whose interests are wholly or largely profits and control.

There is a consideration beyond those of politics and economics. The presence of powerful American corporations creates or perpetuates oppressive social conditions as well. In some countries the needs of profit-oriented companies are placed before the needs of the most desperately poor, sometimes in the hope—never yet realized—that investments can create a rich economy in which also the poor can share. In other countries, such as ultra-racist South Africa, multinationals take advantage of already existing oppression that enhances the business opportunities at good profitability.

The securing and control over sources of raw materials in Third World countries is often exercised and justified by American companies in terms of defense stockpiling. This control process, like the corporate activities discussed above, works to reduce the poor countries to dependence upon the industrialized world. Most of the Third World's resources are exported to the industrialized countries under the auspices of American corporate interests. These countries remain in a semicolonial state, exporting raw materials and depending for their manufacturing products either upon outside sources or domestic sources owned in many instances by multinational corporations. In this state it is ". . . impossible for the people of the Third World to use their resources to fulfill their own needs."[9]

Control of resources by the American multinational institutions is not, however, an isolated phenomenon. It is directly connected to the enormous consumption of goods and services by the American people. Our affluent society absorbs huge quantities of raw materials which benefit a very small and mostly white segment of the world's population. With only six percent of the world's population the United States annually consumes thirty-five percent of the world's energy resources. From this we see that "consumption in the industrialized countries, and especially in the United States, is grossly inordinate and constitutes oppression of the deprived people of the world."[10] To support our overconsumption and affluence, which are inseparable parts of our style of life in white America, we deprive the poor countries of the resources and control that could give them the basis for true and meaningful development. Harry Magdoff points out the international consequences:

> The exploitation of the Third World national and regional resources by foreign corporations, with a consequent outflow of profits from the exploited regions, has resulted in a vast and growing economic disparity among nations and a monopoly of industrialized countries over production, energy, technology, information, and political power.[11]

The overwhelming evidence now available from the Third World is that the white-run, American-controlled and owned, multinational institutions have not helped in any significant way the life and well-being of the lowest sixty to seventy-five percent of the population of the Third World. Industrialization and development may help the elite or most affluent groups within these countries. But the end result for the rest of the population is exploitation and dependency.

In any particular time or place an American international institution may not appear to be oppressive. But as we noted, we must see these political, military, and economic interests in terms of how they actually *work*—as an integrated system. There are no resolvable conflicts between the various branches of our multinational web. They help *each other:*

> As is so often the case, economic interests harmonize comfortably with political and security goals. . . . Quite understandably, the government makes its contribution to the security of the nation as well as to the security of business via diplomatic maneuvers, maintenance of convenient military bases in various parts of the world, military aid to help maintain stable governments, and last but not least a foreign aid program which is a fine blend of declared humanitarian aims and a realistic appreciation that such progress should not interfere with the ability of the supplying countries to maintain a proper flow of raw materials (and profits).[12]

In that monolith of power and control lie the roots of oppression of powerless peoples in poor countries. The compelling dynamism of these institutions is both attractive to those who have nothing and efficient for those who have everything.

OPPRESSION: A WAY OF LIFE

The unmistakable, repeated patterns of oppression are rooted in our lifestyle, society, and culture. The simplest element in that oppression is the key element—we have *profited* from the perpetuation of injustice. Not only are whites alone "on top."

We have also built a system that keeps us there. The paternalism and exploitation that Third World peoples feel is as much a part of our "way of life" as the prosperity, privileges, and benefits we whites enjoy and pursue. To a large extent, we have all that we enjoy only because of the oppression in which we participate. We have done many charitable, positive, and beneficent acts in a world of need; we are not "all bad." But we cannot evade the other half of the truth: we have fed ourselves off the continuing poverty of the world's masses and have exploited the powerless to our own gain.

Most Americans would not be proud of being racist, nor be openly in favor of a racist system. However, we do not have to be bigots to be racists:

> To speak of white racism in America does not mean that everyone who is white believes that the white man possesses some innate superiority. It does mean that American society *operates* as though this were the case, that the *nature* of American society is the same *as if* this belief were held by all whites. One must look at the gross effects of the society's institutions and activities to understand that regardless of individual exception, the total effect of this society is comparable to that of a society based on the ideology of white supremacy.[13]

Similarly, many white Americans would not support open and deliberate exploitation of the Third World. But we do not need to be open and deliberate to oppress:

> The chains of dependence may be manipulated by the political, financial and military arms of the centers of empire, with the help of the Marines, military bases, bribery, CIA operations, financial maneuvers, and the like. But the material basis of this dependence is an industrial and financial structure which through the so-called normal operations of the marketplace reproduces the conditions of economic dependence.[14]

When we examine ourselves as whites and all that we stand for in the world today, we find a paradox. We are not what we suppose ourselves to be. We have fancied ourselves the good guys who make a few mistakes. But that is not what we find. And even while we luxuriate in the relative privilege of finding out what we are not, many suffer the injustices of oppression and exploitation because of what we are.

"What we are" is defined by whiteness and maleness and heterosexual preference. In this chapter we have discussed the meaning of whiteness. Straight white males must recognize that the social structures, political institutions, and economic systems which they control as whites are oppressive. Any steps toward straight white male "liberation" must deal radically with the oppression rooted in these realities; idealistic theorizing is not enough. The oppressed will not accept good-sounding rhetoric of "liberation for all" from the mouths of those who still participate in or benefit from oppressive structures.

NOTES

1. Louis L. Knowles and Kenneth Prewitt, eds., *Institutional Racism in America* (Englewood Cliffs, N.J.: Prentice Hall, 1969), p. 119.
2. Ibid., p. 14.
3. Peter Schrag, *The Decline of the WASP* (New York: Simon & Schuster, 1971), p. 226.
4. Knowles and Prewitt, *Institutional Racism*, p. 4.
5. Ibid., p. 125.
6. Barry N. Schwartz and Robert Disch, eds., *White Racism: Its History, Pathology and Practice* (New York: Dell, 1970), p. 4.
7. Tom Artin, *Earth Talk: Independent Voices on the Environment* (New York: Grossman, 1973), p. 57.
8. Harry Magdoff, "The Age of Imperialism" (New York: Monthly Review, 1969), pp. 20–21. Copyright 1969 by Harry Magdoff; 1966, 1968 by Monthly Review, Inc.
9. Ibid., p. 172.
10. Ibid., p. 117.
11. Ibid., pp. 170–71.
12. Ibid., pp. 196–97.
13. Schwartz and Disch, *White Racism*, p. 65.
14. Magdoff, "Age of Imperialism," p. 198.

Compassion for the suicidal impulse in our killers? Well,
on a plane ride once, the man across the aisle,
who was a World War Two paraplegic,
dead totally from the waist down,
wheeled in and out of the cabin, spent the whole trip avidly
devouring first newspaper sports pages
and then sports magazines,
loudly pointing out to anyone who would listen
(mostly the stewardesses) which athlete was a "real man."
Two men in the seats directly behind me talked the whole time
about which Caribbean islands were the best for whoring, and
which color of ass was hotter and more pliant.
The stewardess smiled and served them coffee.
I gripped the arms of my seat more than once
to stop my getting up and screaming to the entire planeload
of human beings what was torturing us all—stopped
because I knew they'd take me for a crazy, an incipient
hijacker perhaps, and wrestle me down until Bellevue Hospital
could receive me at our landing in New York.*

—Robin Morgan

8.   Maleness and Heterosexuality

Charles E. Lindner

CRITICAL COLLECTIVE CONSCIOUSNESS
Straight white males have paid little critical attention to themselves. What it means to be a straight white male has been of
minor importance historically. Indeed, questions about the
meaning of maleness have been of recent vintage and rarely more
than superficial in content. Liberals of the sixties conducted a
cursory self-review, but were limited by the belief that their
search was for the unique white male virtues needed by various
social marginales.
    The great liberal thesis (of the "Great Society") was built on

the concept that black people would attain "equality" (social, economic, political) if *given* equal educational opportunities, the vote, and chances to compete for a variety of career options. The reemergence of feminism challenged some liberals to readjust their quotas and proclamations. Therapy was prescribed for "sick" gay people; therefore there was no need to modify further the liberal thesis in light of a vocal and visible gay presence.

With a few individual exceptions straight white males have not transcended (if they ever came as far as attaining) the paternalistic style of liberalism. Straightness, whiteness, and maleness still constitute the norm, and "mainstream" American life remains the exclusive property of those who have white skin, are straight in their sexuality, and happen to have male genitals. Essentially, liberal "equality" meant the equal opportunity to be a living apology for one's race and/or sexuality and/or gender. The liberal thesis was deeply rooted in racism, sexism, and straightness. It aimed at a muted form of equality, rather than at justice and liberation from the oppressor-oppressed polarity.

If we are to look at maleness in a manner that goes beyond the flaws of liberalism, we must adopt a perspective attuned to the views of reality articulated by the oppressed. What liberals saw as a melting-pot society, we recognize as a society in which the primary reality is the oppressor-oppressed polarity. *Liberation*, therefore, not equality, must become the focal point of our discussion. What it means to be a male is the fruit of the total experience of oppressorhood. Maleness is rooted in sexism and straightness. For some, the perspective roughly outlined will seem self-evident, indeed even simplistic. But for most males these are alien concepts. At the center of maleness is the experience of oppressorhood, yet male self-consciousness seldom includes such a collective identity. In recent years this violent *un*-consciousness has been confronted by its victims. Only a few straight males have adopted a critical, collective consciousness. To embark on a discussion of maleness, then, is to *begin* the task of straight male consciousness-raising.

Straight male collective self-images are affirmed at only the most unsophisticated level. A combination of pioneer, warrior, entrepreneur, and missionary composes the picture of the American male—as seen by himself. Peter Schrag captures well the spirit of this collective image:

> He was our man. The all-purpose, real-life, bigger-than-life, wide-screen three-dimensional stereophonic composite amal-

gamated now-and-forever certified American. Our man. Who built the country and held it together, who was what every immigrant was supposed to be and every healthy boy to idolize, who spoke plain, fought fair, worked hard, and feared God.[1]

That males were deluded in this common identity has been mentioned previously. To come to terms with oppressorhood, males must construct a collective identity more responsible to reality than fantasy, and understand the processes that have shaped their character.

The first task of male consciousness-raising, then, is to identify the common values and personality characteristics that compose our normative conception of masculinity. On an interpersonal and institutional level, men are victims-products-benefactors of what is culturally understood to be typically male. Political, economic, and social roles of oppressorhood are rooted in this collective consciousness. With the exception of Schrag's "our man," males conceive of themselves in an individualistic sense. They resist the absurd suggestion that male success is the product of conformity to normative masculinity.

Ironically, highly competitive individualism is central to the collective male self-concept. Power over people, situations, and family are components of maleness related to competitive individualism. Likewise, normative masculine sexual styles are aggressive, dominant, possessive, and straight, reflecting a defensive need for situational control and emotional limits.

Maleness is calculating and cerebral. Emotional awareness, verbalization, and behavior are undeveloped and suppressed, in contrast to the extensive nurture of male intellectual and physical capacities. Technical-productive qualities are prized. Creative-artistic qualities are denigrated.

Power obsessiveness, realistic nonemotive thinking, and competitive individualism shape the political styles of masculinity. Violence, dishonesty, hidden agendas, and self-interest are the foremost characteristics of male political roles. Masculine economic prototypes are similar. The "real" world of male capitalistic enterprises sets few limits on tactics and strategies acceptable in accumulating economic power and security.

Normative masculinity concerns itself with man's most intimate relationships. The paradigm of male virtue is the "family man." That single males are inferior persons is manifest in corporate pressures for their "top-men" to present a proper family image. It is expected that any normal man will aspire to and fulfill the nuclear familial roles of breadwinner, head of the family, husband, and father.

Each man's career and family life are the ultimate indicators of his masculinity. The worth of a male is measured by self and others on the basis of success standards related to these aspects of his life. Economic power, personal wealth, political power, professional status, straight sexual prowess, and control over the family are indices of normative masculinity. The major "public" and "private" components of the common male identity are those complexes of attitudes and roles involved in being a "career man" and a "family man." Our work on a critical collective male consciousness, then, will center on unpacking the socialization process and implications of career and family as the bulwark of male identity.

THE CAREER MAN

Central to normative masculinity is man's understanding of himself as a career being. The answer to questions of identity are always in terms of the work he does. From early childhood, males are socialized to expect a life built around and given meaning by the productive, prestigious work they perform. Boyhood experiences, educational processes, male models, and familial roles function to reinforce career-centered male lifestyles. At the birth of a child proud fathers symbolically pass on the career heritage to their sons: "You're looking at a future President!" More realistic expectations for "junior" (a male term) develop along lines that assume in slightly more modest vocations.

Male childhood toys are prominent examples of the socialization process. Erector sets, toy tractors and trucks, Lincoln Logs, and model kits are masculine toys that emphasize task completion, productivity, and technical skills. Creativity is limited to piecing together predetermined designs, building rectangular forms, and imitating the sounds and action of trucks hauling dirt. The characteristics enhanced by such play are amply rewarded. Satisfaction with the building of a skeletal skyscraper is strongly reinforced by parental compliments and encouragement. Failure to construct recognizable structures is a negative and degrading experience. Parental assurances that "you'll build it next time" complete the lesson that failure to accomplish a technical task is not meeting the norm, that normal male experience is successful in such mechanistic endeavors.

Masculine child play not only emphasizes skill development; it also inculcates attitudes necessary for successful careers. Aggressive, competitive, and physical play is expected and encouraged. Contact sports impress upon a boy the realistic necessity of hurting or being hurt in the interests of winning. Careers are built on each *man's* individual efforts and exercise of power. The individualistic competitive attitudes necessary to operate successfully in the corporate or professional world are nurtured in the sandlot baseball and football games. Physical skills (which translate into power), competitive spirit, and personality politics determine the pecking order in boy's sports. Any boy who has been chosen last, or worse yet after a *girl,* knows the destructive pressures and feelings of male inadequacy.

What "boys don't do" in childhood play also prepares them for career orientation. The message imparted by the negative responses to male play that is passive, emotional, or nonproductive is that these qualities are *less than* masculine. A boy who reads, daydreams, or paints is a "mama's boy" (a sexist label). "Sissies" (another sexist label) play with dolls or have tea parties with their *sisters.* That emotional displays are not proper career-oriented behavior is made clear when *Dad* admonishes Junior: "Do you think I'd have my job very long if I cried every time my boss criticized me?" The harsh peer and parental sanctions against activities and attitudes that do not fit in a masculine job world effectively suppress men's emotive, passive, and creative characteristics, while reinforcing the normative male career concept.

School provides another important segment of the career socialization process. Formal education normally occupies thirteen to twenty of the early years of a man's life. The justification for this vast time commitment is predicated on the assumption that there are multiple professional or corporate career opportunities resulting from extended combinations of letters following one's name.

From the day a male begins kindergarten he is subtly, and sometimes not so subtly, directed to work hard and compete for the grades and recognition necessary for a successful career. The path from sandbox to tracking systems, to college preparatory programs to college is not valued intrinsically. Neither is the second or third sheepskin valued particularly for the educational experience it represents. Rather, its importance is derived from the career status demarcation between white and blue collars. Having completed the classic seventeen-year career de-

velopment program, the college graduate chooses the fertile
ground of graduate studies and professionalism, or the good green
world of business. Through such a process, males come to think
of themselves even more fully in terms of the career mold. They
also learn essential skills and attitudes of conformity to institutional processes, goal orientation, and competitive achievement
abilities.

Schools provide an effective microcosm of the career environment. In fact, some educators justify their more rigorous and
inhumane practices as realistic preparation for a highly competitive, achievement-oriented, and individualistic work world.
Grading systems, elitist scholastic organizations, sports competi-
tions, and school government posts provide an effective acculturation procedure for the values, attitudes, and styles necessary to
build successful vocations. Artistic-creative course work that
encourages worldviews less functional in the corporate world is
given low priority and status. That is no mystery! Indeed, the
highschool pecking order is determinative of who has what
economic and educational options. In turn, the status of the
college and one's position within that order determines the entry
point a *man* has into the career world. The system of education,
then, serves to inculcate normative career values into male consciousness by imitating business pressures, by projecting the values of career capitalism onto male students, and by dispensing
access to prestigious careers on the basis of achievements.

The effect of schools on male self-perceptions is as profound as
it is designed to be. The most eloquent, yet ironic, testimony to
the career-education connection is the current crisis in higher
education. Enrollment in college is plummeting as a result of the
declining market value of a college education. The overall implications for career socialization and its relation to education are
unclear. But by virtue of systemic inertia educational institutions continue to influence males to consider themselves career
beings.

Models of maleness also serve in the formation of masculine
self-images. Socialization via model occurs on two significant
levels: through the language used to describe and assess males,
and by identification with important male figures in one's personal
experience. Males are identified and judged in the language that
describes their career status and competency. Indeed, when
males speak autobiographically they move directly to the nitty-
gritty: how they make their living. Boys listening to conversa-

tions equating men with what they do, and how they do it, learn central truths about normative masculine traits. The tone and adjectives surrounding discussions of unemployment, firings, or bankruptcy reflect the degradation and male inadequacy of career problems. Through the language of job descriptions, paradigms of successful and inadequate men are revealed.

Of immeasurable impact is the influence of male figures in a man's life. Male models available to boys in their identity development run the range of careers! Starting with the deep impression of Dad as an absentee figure due to his work, male children encounter few men who fail to conform to a life centered on career paradigms. Males soon discern that there is a clear hierarchy of prestige and income revealed in the blue collar/white collar/executive-professional stratification. Doctors and lawyers are near deity in status, while factory workers, laborers, and garbage*men* are known to be of inferior human potential. Such distinctions clarify the lesson that males of human worth are involved in income-producing, nondomestic, full-time, important work, and that work is the center of their lives.

Through this examination of male career socialization, part of the framework of a collective male story is established. It is the common experience of men to be socialized into the competitive, aggressive, individualistic attitudes necessary to build a career in a society that considers those character traits to be superior. Furthermore, it is the collective experience of males to be psychologically dependent upon their career success for satisfaction and a positive self-image. A major contribution to a critical collective male consciousness, then, is this recognition that straight males are psychologically dependent upon their status as oppressor. The institutions and economy that create careers and meaning for straight males are the primary instruments of oppression. The drive for successful careers is a dynamic force in sustaining institutional racism and sexism.

Males find themselves at once to be the victims, products, and beneficiaries of careerism's connections with sexism and racism. Male identification with the careerism ethic is a product of the socialization experience of males in our white paternalistic culture. As products of these systems, men are the manipulators of power in all aspects of American culture. Indeed, their status as beneficiaries involves not only material gains but also the psychological satisfactions that go with "success." But men too are the dehumanized victims of their own oppressorhood. The emotive, creative, and passive qualities of males are crushed in their earliest years. Perhaps more seriously, men are possessed by their demonic experience of psychological dependence on the oppression of people.

THE FAMILY MAN

The rigidity of normative masculinity intensifies in the realm of sexuality. Indeed, the economic, social, and legal sanctions against those who "deviate" from the norm are severe. Gay people find themselves victims of job discrimination, and are relegated to the social status of pervert and the legal position of outlaw. The story of how males become "family men" is the outline of the socialization of men into straightness and sexism on an interpersonal level.

The story of straightness originates with male alienation from physical pleasure experienced alone. Simultaneous with an infant's discovery of his genitals is the realization that his parents disapprove of genital play. The best of parents distract the child, while the worst react in disgust and rejection. In both cases it is presupposed that for a child to play with his genitals is wrong. As the young male matures, attitudes of shame, disgust, and fear surround his masturbation. Clearly irrational scare tactics, such as the multiple consequences of sterility, blindness, madness, and homosexuality, are employed by parents to inhibit masturbation. While few males accept the literal truth of such statements, they incorporate the fundamental attitude that onanistic behavior is unnatural and perverted. Initial male sexual experiences, then, represent a conflict between physical pleasure and their perceptions of the immoral nature of masturbation.

Further alienating males from their genital pleasures and experiences is the pubescent "wet dream." Again, parental influence ranges from relatively enlightened preparation to no conversations whatsoever. For most males it is another alienating experience. Males develop a sense of their genitals functioning independently of and often against their wishes. Coupled with the cultural myth that males have powerful and, at times, uncontrollable sexual desires, the young male perceives his sexual makeup to be separate from his rationality. It is as if sexuality is a remnant of animal nature that requires all of a male's "higher" resources to control. Men's most fundamental sexual experiences—with themselves—are characterized by intellectual and emotional alienation from physical pleasure.

In part because of this conflict, sexuality is most generally conceived of in terms of relationship to others. But excluded from that general concept are homosexual relationships. Again, the straight male story begins in childhood. Parents will, on occasion, discover little boys playing with each other's genitals. The reaction is similar to parental responses to masturbation. A negative response is assumed, and its harshness ranges to hysterical extremes. Reinforcing such specific experiences is the absence of models of male-male physical affection. The oppressed status of gay people limits the possibility of positive exposure to gay lifestyles. Even Dad is sparing in physical affection past infancy as the father-son relationship becomes a nonphysical companionship or degenerates into the authority model. Indeed, postinfancy physical contact between fathers and sons is often limited to handshakes and spankings!

Peer relationships provide major input in socializing males into normative masculine concepts of sexuality. Collective ignorance informs the derisive attitudes of boyhood peers toward gays. Fear of that which is unknown is reinforced by the prejudices of the dominant culture in creating a sexual identity that finds traces of homosexuality threatening. Signs of passivity, affective behavior toward another male, and so-called feminine gestures are traits that threaten the masculinity of the peer group and are, in turn, used to assault the "manliness" of the nonconforming member. When, on occasion, close friends or brothers engage in some level of sexual relationship, it becomes a secretive experience that haunts the participant. The dynamics of the male peer group serve to suppress not only verbal and physical expressions of affection, but also the passive, emotive, creative traits of males that are viewed as symptoms of a disgusting perverted sickness.

The straight male self-image responds to the possibility of being gay with much the same dread one feels toward suffering through a terminal illness. Fundamental to straight male self-respect is a well-armored confidence in one's heterosexuality. As a result, males face prohibitive social and psychological pressures if they adopt traits considered feminine. Men find it even more problematic to express the deep affection they often feel for each other. Straightness complements careerism by similarly suppressing emotive, passive, and creative elements in male personalities. Again, in repressing homosexuality, males are alienated from physical and emotional experiences that they regard as unnatural.

Finding the fulfillment of male-male relationships excluded from normative masculine sexuality, straight male relationships with women are the remaining realm of acceptable sexuality. The burden of emotional expression falls exclusively on male-female relationships, but in a manner that further dehumanizes those involved. Heterosexuality is characterized by possessiveness, female objectification, and a series of roles assigned by sex such as male initiator–female passive object.

Male childhood experience with females is characterized by a rigid separatism. A review of the distinctions between "boys' play" and "girls' play" reveals the formation of male attitudes regarding females. Boys disdain girls' forms of entertainment, asserting the superiority of baseball, building forts, and catching frogs over the domestic quality of playing house and having tea parties. The logic is flawless: no girl can play second base, but any boy can play with dolls! Or so it seems.

Family experiences function to substantiate the boyhood assessment of the worth of girls. Girls wash dishes, do dusting, and vacuum floors, while boys rake leaves, shovel snow, and mow grass. The actors are interchangeable in only one direction: boys can do girls' work, but girls can't do boys' jobs. Two essential lessons are learned through the divisions of work and play: boys are superior to girls, and there is no basis for boys and girls to spend time together because girls are useless to boys. The *object* lesson has just begun!

The attitudinal framework of childhood that females are objects evaluated on a utility basis is applied to new data with the onset of puberty. The same parents and peers who had supported the separatism of prepubescence, now support the social integration of the sexes. With the development of mature bodies, females' usefulness is revealed. The fundamental principle giving purpose to male-female relationships is the attitude that women are sex objects.

The social-sexual institution of dating provides the setting for males to learn further essential attitudes of normative masculinity. Dating is structured around the basic roles of man-the-initiator and woman-the-passive-object. In preparation for "asking for a date" males conduct something akin to an investment analysis. Various objects are evaluated on the basis of appearance, "reputation," passivity, and whether an initiative would receive an affirmative response. It is an understatement to conclude that dating is sexist. The influence of dating on the normative masculine self-concept is significant. The dramatic psycho-dynamics of "asking for a date" reflect the importance for a positive male self-image of success at initiator roles. Few males relish their memories of the agony of uncertainty and failure in dating. Once again, it is clear that males are psychologically dependent upon success in fulfilling an inherently oppressive role.

Trapped within the dehumanizing structure of dating, males and females are unable to develop simple friendships and deep and rewarding intellectual, emotional, and physical relationships that retain their mutual dignity. The major product of the dating syndrome is a perverted concept of male-female love, popularly known as "romance." Characterized by male dominance, possessiveness, and obsessive privacy, romances are inward and exclusive relationships. In the context of romance, men begin to feel security in verbal and physical expressions of their emotions. Because there is a sense of ownership of property, rather than trust, men feel safe in vulnerability within the structure of romance. With the possibility of emotional involvement limited to romance, there is an overload of expectations and needs heaped on the "couple" involved.

Romance is the singular experience where a man breaks through the radical loneliness of competitive individualism. Indeed, the whole rat race derives its meaning from its connection with the institutionalized form of romance—marriage. While normative masculinity makes career the source of a positive sense of self, it brings fulfillment and pleasure to life through marriage and family. Male identity is given its human character through family life. Otherwise men would simply be economic functionaries.

Male visions of marriage are of a haven where the competitive individualism of the workday is left behind. Being a husband means primarily an economic role as breadwinner and a political role as head of the household. As a good career man the husband provides home, food, clothes, and luxuries for his fragile wife. In return, his emotional, sexual, and spiritual needs are met after a long day's work. Career life for the single man means a rugged existence, as it is costly to pay for a cook, maid, prostitute, and analyst.

Of course any happy marriage becomes a happy family! Every man wants a little princess and a robust son. Not only does it give his wife fulfillment; it is also important to be a father. As a father you get all the joys of having children, but none of the responsibilities! The thrill of vicarious success through your *son*'s achievements, the ego rewards of an adoring daughter are satisfactions found only in the family. Marriage and the family meet vital emotional and psychological needs of the career man. Without an oppressed wife, much of the meaning of a man's existence would be absent.

The collective male story of the family man is a process of eliminating options for emotive expression and sexuality. Normative masculinity drastically delimits the possibility of full human relationships. Male-male interactions are confined to jocular and intellectual companionship that is terrified of emotional or sexual expressions. Male-female relationships are formed initially, after years of separatism, in the context of dating. The normative progression from dating is into romance, marriage, and family. The path of male relationships with women is from radical loneliness to exclusive monogamy. Marriage fulfills man's roles of initiator, breadwinner, and dominant figure over women as well as providing the psychological and spiritual support absent in the single life.

The family is also a key economic unit in wasteful American consumerism. On any given block in the suburbs the total technology, energy, food, and building materials consumed far exceed the human needs. That the American standard of living is a criminal reality in a world of poverty and hunger is directly related to nuclear family consumerism. The oppression that males benefit from in their family life is not only that of their wives, but also the poverty of the Third World.

Males are dependent upon the family for the servicing of their psychological needs for affective relationships. The American nuclear family represents the cornerstone of female oppression. Furthermore, it is the consumer unit that is the primary beneficiary of the inequitable distribution of resources in the world. Normative masculinity is a lifestyle that cannot exist in its present form without the benefits of oppressorhood.

The picture is even more complex. Men are not only, if primarily, beneficiaries of the status quo; they are also its victims and products. In the same manner as careerism, males are victims of the demonic experience of psychological dependency on the oppression of women and gays. As straight males, they are also victims of the denial of full relationships with men and women outside of monogamy. Indeed, even the holy institution of matrimony is more accurately characterized by possessiveness, sexism, and exclusivity than by trust, love, respect, and openness. In the tensions of the split identity of beneficiary-victim-product, the straight white male comes to awareness and seeks liberation.

STORY AND PRAXIS

The career and family aspects of the normative masculine story represent major portions of the "public" and "private" lives of straight white males. That career and family appear in individualized forms obscures, but does not contradict, the collective nature of this story. Analysis of the story of maleness, in light of its connections with the structures of oppression, helps to reveal the roots of collective male identity in oppressorhood. Males derive meaning and purpose from a status quo that oppresses, and therefore, find their mundane self-interests of career and family in conflict with the agenda of human liberation. If the agenda of liberation includes fundamental changes in the career world, the elimination of the oppressive divisions of masculine and feminine, and radical change in the style, shape, and character of family, then the story of maleness runs in direct conflict with liberation.

Straight white males have paid little critical attention to themselves! When confronted with the liberation movements of the world, the oppressors move to protect their positions. But there is another option. That is to continue our task of critical self-analysis and move to praxis. The agenda of straight white male liberation begins with assembling the collective story of the oppressor. From a sense of what it means to be a straight white male, the process moves to identifying lifestyles that seek to eliminate participation in the systems of oppression. To the fullest extent possible straight white males must restructure their identities and reroot themselves in a way of life that is not dependent upon the benefits of the status quo. In essence, the path of liberation goes from story to praxis again and again. It is a process that seeks to move beyond the tensions of victim-product-beneficiary of the oppressor-oppressed polarity.

NOTES

*Robin Morgan, "Monster," from *Monster: Poems by Robin Morgan* (New York: Vintage Books, 1972), pp. 83–84. Copyright © 1972 by Robin Morgan. Reprinted by permission of Random House, Inc.

1. Peter Schrag, *The Decline of the WASP* (New York: Simon & Schuster, 1971), p. 13.

Part Four

Toward Whiteness, Maleness, and Sexuality in a New Perspective: A Dialogue

O God, RAZE my consciousness. Amen.*

9. Liberation for Straight White Males

Glenn R. Bucher and Charles E. Lindner

The dialogue which constitutes chapters 9 and 10 is a response to the previous chapters in this book and an effort to go beyond them in the direction of liberation for straight white males. The dialogue brings together the two most traditionally socialized straight white male contributors to the volume, Glenn R. Bucher and Charles E. Lindner. The discussion between them occurred after prior wrestling with the materials of all the contributors. It was recorded on tape and subsequently transposed and edited by Glenn R. Bucher.

STORYTELLING
B: As I see it, there are two possible straight white male responses to the liberation struggles of blacks, women, homosexuals, and movements in the Third World. One is to react against them, to insist that they are "fringe movements," to insist that what "the minorities" are saying either is not true or pertains only to them; this is not a desirable option in my mind. The other response is to be sympathetic and open to those struggles and to their implications for straight white males.

L: Of course, the *fringes* of straight white male Western society are much larger than the so-called mainstream. The voices of protest come from the world's majority, corporately considered. So the idea of fringe makes sense only in that these people are on the fringes of power.

114

B: That's one of the reasons why the reaction I mentioned is uninformed.   Still, straight white males will have a tough time understanding that, numerically, they are an insignificant group in the world community.

L: What about the argument that since blacks, women, and homosexuals are, within the U.S., on the fringes of power, they aren't worth taking seriously?   The opposite response—the appropriate one I think—is to say that for straight white male identity to be legitimate, it must be worked out amidst the pluralistic realities we know exist.   But most straight white males are very parochial.   Some have argued that "the minorities" need help getting into "the mainstream."   But I think we need to move beyond parochialism and the missionary spirit; the mainstream *is* the problem!   It is cut off from the larger "fringes," yet dictates the economic, social, and political realities for all the world.

B: Speaking of straight white males being in the mainstream, some blacks, women, and homosexuals argue that since we are so much a part of the status quo, we can't achieve perspective enough even to talk about our own liberation.   I'm sympathetic to that response but not intimidated by it.   I think we *can* move in a creative direction toward liberation, even though part of our freedom will come through the struggles of others.

L: I can put it even more emphatically: We *want* some changes in our own lives and we *don't* want to wait.

B: Precisely!

L: That's what blacks, women, and homosexuals want too. One aspect of their struggles has been a kind of storytelling.   In talking together among themselves, they have discovered many common experiences.   I think straight white males can take a cue from that.

B: How can storytelling help?   What do you mean by storytelling?

L: To be personal, I mean that because the two of us are straight white males our individual histories intersect at interesting points.   In sharing past experiences we have discovered that our self-images have been shattered in similar ways.   You and I have even been involved in the same community-living experience.   So our discussions here are built on shared ground, but ground that goes beyond simply the two of us.   I think that we and other persons like us must and can tell our collective story to one another.

B: Our personal chronologies are important too.   Had it not been for my involvement in the black struggle, I would not have begun to think in the ways I have. I was forced to face whiteness, and eventually I began to consider sexuality and sexual preference. But it was the black struggle that triggered my thinking about my own past and the kinds of socializations my story revealed. Then I discovered other straight white males who were interested in exploring their past as well and we saw common areas in our emerged individual stories. I concluded that straight white males have a great deal to share.

L: The crucial experience for me was hitting the college campus just when many of the movements of the sixties, particularly those revolving around Vietnam, were prominent. These brought to consciousness problems inherent in my American dream. Then there were black-white confrontations. Finally, I encountered women committed to feminism. This culminated in a realization that the problem of oppression in the world is directly linked to straight white males. As a senior in college facing vocational options, I decided to work for a year in an upper-middle-class white suburban community as typically American as apple pie. Now I live in New York City, where daily I'm confronted by many reminders that my straightness, my whiteness, and my maleness are not normative for others. What is important is that you and I have both gone through, and continue to encounter, experiences that shatter the illusions by which we once lived, and we reject reactionary responses which try to patch up or defend those illusions.

B: The main thing now, the only thing that is human and responsible in these circumstances, is to work on our own liberation. An important part of this process clearly involves straight white males telling their own story, because they need to hear what it is. It is one thing to know it intellectually, but another to articulate it aloud.

L: The idea of collective story is particularly important because we Americans don't generally see our society as polarized into social groups. We tend to think rather in individualistic terms. But to talk about straight white males having a common story is to begin to be sensitive to the group. Just as blacks, women, and homosexuals feel a group identity, so straight white males are, on the world scene, a group with a common history, whether we recognize it or not. We have a collective identity which is implicated in the liberation movements—or oppressions—of others.

B: One of the values of the storytelling, then, is that others like us can hear and see their stories in ours.

L: Yes, the straight white male story reveals a common socialization pattern.   And that's important to be aware of, because there *is* a set of values and attitudes that we are taught and on the basis of which we assume certain roles, and we're learning only now that those roles are oppressive for others.   Our collective identity is, in one sense, that of oppressorhood.   Most of us don't understand this.   To talk about story is to discover and to examine our corporate assumptions, and to see how straight white males view the world in the same way.

B: Straightness, whiteness, and maleness are not equivalent to WASPness, but they're connected to it, and the WASP has received considerable attention in sociological study.   Maybe it's easier for straight white males to get hold of who they are if they think in terms of WASP culture, a phenomenon that is visible in American society and clearly identified with power and social control.   Perhaps the notion of WASPness will enable us to go back to straightness, whiteness, and maleness and understand them as a collective reality.

L: Thanks to storytelling we're learning about the common experiences that have formed us as individuals and established our roots.   We also learn of the myths and beliefs by which we live, such things as the American dream, the nuclear family, the successful career, and the power and control you mentioned.

B: Something I discovered in thinking about my story—and telling it—was that American culture is not uniform.   There are different sides to it.   As long as I was only exposed within it—and not observant of it—my basic assumptions were not challenged. Education only challenged me to fulfill my American dream. Liberalism forced me to adjust some of the myths, but it didn't give a radical critique of them.   The idea that through education one can gain an accurate understanding of the world is itself a myth, for there are clear limits to what middle-class education can do.   That's because the educational institutions and goals presuppose the normativeness of Middle-American culture.

L: That's an important point.   Why is it that while we were growing up we didn't ask many questions about the straight white male world view?   Probably, as you said, because we didn't have enough perspective or experience.   People living in areas like those in which we grew up don't need to deal daily with blacks, angry women, and homosexuals.   They dwell in the midst of

unassaulting realities. Many can't imagine that anything might
be wrong with their American dreams. Even liberals assume that
they know why social problems exist, and how to interpret the
experience of blacks and others. They even propose formulas
for resolving "minority" problems. Usually these formulas included mainstream America becoming more "aware," and some
good liberal education for the rest so that they too can then dress
properly and talk right, and pursue the goals, values, and careers
acceptable to Middle America.

B: You know I too was/am a liberal, but one problem with
liberals is that often they are prepared to go only to the water's
edge of change, so to speak. At least that's what I now conclude
from looking back at the 1960s. Liberals want to change society
so long as they don't need to change significantly their own lifestyle.

L: That's a negative way of putting it. Let me say that liberals (and some of my best friends are liberals!) don't change their
lifestyles because they think the American pie includes enough
for all. They appeal to progress, ingenuity, government spend-
ing, and so on. That was always my panacea too, but my American dream came apart when I left a rural setting, visited the city
where my brother was working in civil rights, and had my mind
blown. For a time I still believed that more government support,
financial and legal, could resolve the crises. Soon thereafter,
however, my political consciousness was aroused as I watched
the 1968 Democratic Convention in Chicago. I discovered that
police can be violent, excessively violent—something that blacks
had been saying for a long time. And then came Vietnam.

B: It sounds as though part of your story, like mine, includes
"the dream destroyed." How did that happen?

L: Cambodia and Kent State did it. I was involved in the
peace movement out of liberal motivations. I identified that
movement for peace with participatory democracy, only to discover that it didn't work in America: participatory democracy
was a mythical assumption, for the power structures were and are
controlled from the inside. Then, after college, I went to work in
a white suburban community near Detroit where I discovered
many people who continued to live as though the 1967 riots never
happened. I saw the juxtaposition of affluence and poverty. I
saw how young lives even in the midst of affluence were being
destroyed by drugs. That confirmed for me the roots of the problem. I concluded there is something amiss in the dreams and
lifestyles by which many WASP Americans live.

B: So our dreams have been inherited, challenged, and then destroyed. What does that leave us with? Where do we go from here?

L: I think we begin by going back to our stories and looking at straightness, whiteness, and maleness.

SEPARATION

B: Perhaps so, but before we pick up on that, I think we need to tell our readers something they probably want to know: Why are the two of us—straight white males—doing these final chapters alone? Our answer, I think, relates to the storytelling we just discussed.

L: Yes, some will insist we are avoiding a confrontation. It's true: even our other contributors can't challenge us because we are isolated here. But we are also trying to take seriously the very point they all have made—that straight white males are off by themselves in a place they have themselves created. If we take their indictment seriously, then we must for a change, and as a beginning—*recognize* that we are cut off. There *is* social polarity. We have nurtured the situation in which separation is real. Now we must work out part of our liberation in that context.

B: Others will accuse us of *using* a black, a woman, and a homosexual to initiate our own struggle, and then cutting them out at the end. But I'm glad this symposium is not ending with six people sitting down, holding hands, and talking about how we can all be human together. I once thought that would be an ideal concluding format. But I changed my mind. I don't think the times permit that—yet.

L: And I don't want to be asking the typical question: What do you think we straight white males ought to do? That takes energy and time; it uses people. We have heard from Berry, Hill, and Gaver. We listened to them, I hope. We recognize the conflicts. We heard their message: These are not polite times. . . . Straight white males created the situation. . . . There are no easy solutions; reconciliation will not be achieved quickly or easily. Hence, we must talk together alone. We must speak among ourselves of the conflicts and radical polarization. If the oppressor-oppressed categories make any sense, then we stand on one side of that dichotomy—we are the oppressors.

B: We also recognize that liberation is a process requiring both separation and community. But what do these words really mean; when should those events happen, and in what order? I think that before we can talk of corporate and liberated community, we must face the fact of separation. We are acknowledging that here and now. We were not forced to be alone. Berry, Hill, and Gaver were willing to be with us. In other words, they see their oppression in a larger context that includes our dehumanization as well. At the same time, they were prepared to grant us the time and space to be alone. We must move through the same process they are involved in. Culturally, this doesn't seem to be the right time to be with them.

L: Are we doing this discussion because we feel guilty? or to avoid guilt? or to resolve it? I think we definitely feel guilt because we recognize how as straight white males we are responsible for others' situations. That fact must be faced squarely. But this relates to another of the criticisms to which we may be vulnerable. Some will say those straight white males are guilty and hurting and want to make others feel the same way. We must ask: how much can guilt actually motivate us?

B: Clearly, there are limits to the potential creativity in guilt. But guilt is a good thing in the sense that it is one response to seeing interconnections between the stories of blacks, women, homosexuals, and our own story. To see the consequences of those connections is to be ashamed. Maybe that's a good sign, even if it's not the final sign. Not to feel guilty in face of the facts is not to be sensitive. But we must ask: how long can we dwell on guilt? how can it be imaginatively used?

L: We also came together because we believe straight white males can do something for themselves. We can affirm a kind of liberation from the polarities already mentioned. We can look at our end of the polarity, and there be transformed.

B: True! But what are the cues for what we need to do? If our dreams are destroyed, if we are implicated in others' hurts, if we feel guilty, if there seems to be no past upon which to draw, and no other persons either, then we are left with ourselves. Upon what are we to build?

L: While we say part of the American dream is meaningless for us, while we disavow many of the things it represents, we continue to live it. Yet an alternative to that dream is what we seek, and in terms of heritage—while heritage remains a problem in the mainstream sense—we are not without supportive histories outside of ourselves.

B: I guess we're also saying that our claim on humanness guarantees us a bit of freedom to rise above and transcend the past. We are not immobilized by what we have been made to be. We think we can push beyond that. Our being able to move is based on hope.

L: We can talk about hope if we want, as well as about transcendence and creative movement. But let's not forget that *all* of that—liberation, I mean—must eventuate in concrete work; our lives must change.

B: OK, let's get more concrete, though I suspect it will be difficult!

LIBERATION

B: What do we mean by liberation? Rather than talk theoretically about what it is, can we speak in fact about oppression? What I have in mind is that we have heard from the oppressed. Our own story exposes dehumanization. Maybe to get to liberation we must go through the back door of oppression. Of course, oppression is a back door only for those who don't experience it firsthand.

L: I think we can talk about what reality is as we see it. The oppressed have a perspective on reality. And what we know about those social realities is that we stand on one side. I think we see that clearly. The nature of liberation has to do with attempting to break down that polarity. That means change. It doesn't mean that straight white males can say they are oppressed. We don't want to deny the pain and dehumanization we feel. Straight white male identity is a problem for us and others. But for straight white males to say that they are oppressed makes nonsense out of the oppressed-oppressor truth. The first thing to say about liberation is that concrete historical circumstances have to be changed. Structures of domination exist, maintained by people like us. Liberation means changing what exists in the world.

B: Some straight white males will disclaim maintaining those structures. To them I say: you benefit from them! We are talking not only of intentional manipulation, but of how straight white males also profit through default. That is more pervasive and more subtle!

L: Until those structures of domination are gone, I don't believe straight white males will be able to change on their own. The oppressed are saying those structures must and can be changed from the bottom up. Straight white males can recognize in the structures the interconnections between themselves and the oppressed. Liberation for us, then, will mean the renunciation of some things. We must begin by saying no to some of the connections, by not accepting the benefits available to us. We can become less dependent upon the oppression of others for our meaning, our existence, and all that makes us what and who we are. I'm speaking of a kind of breaking off from what is available to us. Total separation is not possible, of course. We are stuck with being oppressors, and probably wonder whether we can ever do anything much about it. But there are aspects of our complicity which need not be. We can change.

B: Can we be more explicit about liberation? One way for me to get at it is to see what blacks, women, and homosexuals are saying about liberation.

L: A major point for me in that definition is to talk about *space*. Women and others are saying that they don't want to be defined by straight white males—by their relatedness to us—or by conforming to our patterns. Necessary to their liberation is enough space to exist and live on their own terms, and to develop and nurture a separate, unique identity.

B: Is oppression then not having control over one's space—over who one is—over the power of naming one's history and choices? One must have an independence of operation, it seems. If oppression is not having that power, then liberation is having the power to determine who one is and wants to become—historically, psychically, economically, politically, and socially.

L: For us, that means finding out where we are denying people space, power, and the opportunities to name.

B: Hill talked about that. Do you think what she said would apply to blacks and homosexuals?

L: Of course! In American society today there is a monolith of straight white male values that defines who is successful and happy; who gets what jobs, income, and luxuries; who is middle-class and affluent; who doesn't get any of these. Many are forced to conform to the straight white male style if they want to have personal and social dignity. Straight white males assume that what they do is normal and that others should aspire to normalcy. They seem to know what the essence of the good life is. Usually it's spoken of in terms of economic "success." But this isn't realistic or equitable in a larger context. Think about the consumption of food and energy; about the population explosion. The facts indicate clearly that the resource pie isn't big enough and can't be equitably divided. Not everyone can be affluent. Either there will be basic inequity and polarization, as we now have, or else there will have to be a radical redefinition of what the good life is.

B: This gets to the heart of the American dream-myth, the presupposition that there is enough for all those who want it.

L: Yes, we tend to believe that progress is unending, that possibilities for economic growth and consumption are open-ended. For straight white males these notions give meaning to their lives. But the point is that to maintain these myths is to increase oppression, because so many stand outside the realm of these unlimited opportunities. And that is a way of saying that straight white male identity is linked to the oppression of others.

B: To retain these values is indeed to increase oppression, because some people must be denied. Traditionally, straight white males have denied these social realities to blacks, women, and homosexuals. At least the facts are clear: as long as there is affluence, there will also be oppression, because there simply is not enough to go around. We are just beginning to discover that—I hope!

L: That suggests to me that one of the fundamental challenges to any notion of liberation relates to defining a more simple level of existence, simple economically and in other ways. Let's face it, the resources are drying up for maintaining the style of life we want and to which we are accustomed.

B: There's an ironical dimension to the matter of affluence. We are saying that straight white males must begin to say no to traditional forms and aspects of affluence—at the same time that many blacks, women, and gays are demanding that way of life.

L: That's a problem, in my view, because these American movements are not connected to Third World struggles among the poor. Because of the inequitable distribution of food 10,000 people starve to death each week. Most of them are in the Third World (Africa, Asia, and Latin America). That's a fact no liberation movement can ignore.

B: Which raises a difficult issue! If there are straight white males in touch with these facts and with Third World liberation movements, can we go to blacks, women, and gays and tell them that unless they are in touch, they too will become oppressors? To do that is for straight white males to fall back into the same old pattern of telling others what they should know and believe and do. Maybe the only thing we can do is talk among ourselves and quit trying to instruct blacks, women, and homosexuals.

Why do I say that? Because we must start saying no, since to say yes is to continue oppression; and because if we speak loudly enough, some others might take notice.

L: If we say no to guaranteed luxuries, we are in a sense answering the Third Worlders now speaking up on their own behalf. There are some clear issues which must be raised for all to see and hear. Straight white males cannot define for others what liberation should mean—the power of definition is a form of oppression. But at the same time, liberation movements must be seen in a world perspective. We cannot overlook this.

B: You say we must watch out that we don't tell the oppressed what they are doing wrong. But why are we so attracted to correcting the mistakes of the oppressed? Is it because straight white males have an easier time articulating the problems than formulating creative solutions?

L: I think so. Even to discuss the question is difficult. It is hard to transcend where straight white males are. I guess we have said, however, that liberation for straight white males starts with us looking at ourselves.

B: Is it a rationalization though to say that one of the most essential points at which to begin liberation is at the point of being in touch with one's dehumanization? That seems rather self-serving.

L: We stand in a difficult position with respect to dehumanization.

B: True! We're talking about being in touch with our own oppressorhood. But this doesn't afflict us daily in unbearable ways. Oppressorhood is, and is not, a reality for us.

L: We benefit from it, and find ourselves comfortable in a world where many aren't. We can say that the road to liberation begins by getting in touch with oppression, but we don't have oppression to get in touch with, not oppression that we can feel, identify, groan under, curse at. What we experience is guilt. We talk about it, and sometimes we equate guilt with oppression, or inflate it into a grand form of dehumanization. Guilt is painful, but the daily guilt of being the oppressor is also terribly comfortable. We are at home, so to speak. We are affluent, eating steaks while others starve. We have split-level homes in a world split between the "haves" and "have nots." Our examination of liberation comes amidst luxuries. On the other hand, the oppressed come to their consciousness through pain, suffering, and the opposite of what we experience. Liberation is far less pressing for us. It's easier to ignore and push away.

B: We are talking about the abnormality of normalcy again. Straight white males are dehumanized, not oppressed. I don't think that's only a linguistic distinction. Oppression is manifest daily in overt ways. It is tangible, immediate, and physical. To say that we are oppressed is nonsense. That is not our problem.

L: Of course not. Oppressorhood is too comfortable. And because oppressorhood is pleasant, we have little perspective on it. This is why guilt can be a good starting point. But guilt can lead to reaction—people get tired of it. To be "dehumanized," however, as the oppressors are, is first of all to be in touch with that dehumanization and this is an intellectual process. First, one finds his dreams threatened or shattered. Perhaps the nuclear family, the successful career, or the advantages of professionalism lose meaning. Or we aren't given enough oil and gasoline to drive our cars. That is, the affluence of our American life is challenged. At that point, the insecurity of the benefits we have starts to surface. And that produces alienation.

B: In one sense our alienation will not come swiftly. On the other hand, the moment we see some of our benefits fade, we know we can do something about defusing the challenges. We have the power, the bombs, and the money. Though we may not regard these responses as legitimate, they certainly are possible solutions.

L: There are also ways to insulate ourselves. We can return to "womb" settings. I have in mind safe, carefully controlled, and comfortable places. Maybe the academic community is one of them. It is not easy to decide today where straight white males interested in liberation should be living. Many questions come to mind. Are there prerequisites for a context which enables liberation to happen? Where can the support we need and the renunciation we seek be nurtured? If we want to step away, so to speak, I think we must move to a setting that supports renunciation, yet one in which the reasons for it are obvious daily.

B: We are saying, somewhat reluctantly I think, that we must be in a place where we are faced with the constant challenges. Can we do this voluntarily?

L: Last year I was in Birmingham, Michigan. Life there is easy and comfortable. The most successful businessmen in America live there. The Third World is far away. While there, I felt I needed touch points to bring me back and give me a critical perspective. So I came to New York City. Straight white males need to be challenged. Though alienated in the suburbs, I felt as though I was sliding backwards in terms of consciousness. There was not much to restore me. On the other hand, in New York City one needs to be cautioned not to become calloused in another way. Normalcy here, in many respects, means oppression. I am saying that straight white males need a context and an environment which feed a critical awareness. And I guess I've said, hopefully with not too much self-righteousness, that straight white males can be purposeful about where they live.

COMING TO CONSCIOUSNESS

B: We've said that straight white males need to be intellectually in touch with the realities of the world, and with how they are implicated in them, as they initiate the task of liberation. It seems so obvious: the world looks different to one who lives on the top of it, as compared with those who live on the bottom. Trying to get these simple facts clear, it seems to me, will facilitate intellectual awareness and consciousness. Unfortunately, straight white males have not heard enough about what much of the rest of the world experiences. The plight of others has not made an impact on our lives. Added to this is the fact that the data we usually receive is prepared and dispensed by people just like us. I'm implying that the resources for locating the facts, and developing a legitimate interpretation of them, are more dependable coming from those who stand least to benefit from arranging them in a comfortable way.

L: Someone is bound to ask, and appropriately: To whom shall I listen, anyway? After all, people get information, and interpretations of it, from many different sources.

B: You're asking how one knows what one knows. Let me put it this way. Though I know a great deal about myself, I don't know everything. Others can tell me things I don't know. Obviously, such information is valuable for an honest assessment of self, and it often comes from critics if one is prepared to seek them out, or listen. What I'm intimating in terms of our discussion is that the critics of the oppressor—the oppressed—are telling us what we haven't heard before. They have facts we need to hear. But I also think the world's victims (incidentally, victims are not necessarily saints) have moral claim on a kind of truth that the victors don't have. From firsthand experience, the oppressed know what I don't. I assume that facts in the service of a potentially-more-human life for all are those that must claim my attention first.

L: Good point! The facts you speak of go beyond the truth

about reality which we have known in straight white male circles. They supersede our worldview and experience. We must listen to blacks, women, homosexuals, and the Third World. Their hard facts are passionate observations. For example, we Americans eat five times more than peoples in the Third World and sixty percent more protein than we need. These facts give us a sense of the human dichotomies in today's world. Having an awareness, however partial, of this larger picture, we can then begin to appropriate the knowledge to, in, and for our own lives.

B: Besides intellectual awareness there must also be a gut level knowledge of dehumanization. I have a variety of things that are integral to being a straight white male in American society: the inability to express emotions publicly, the limitations implicit in the roles of father and husband and head of a nuclear family, the pressures associated with vocational positions and advancement, and the human expectations that others place upon you.

L: Let me add the matter of possessiveness. Straight white males assume that women find their meaning in life via relationships with men. And in many instances, men expect to find meaning in the emotional support women give them. They also take that support for granted. Men seem to have the idea that they are secure because women are dependent. My conclusion is that being the possessor carries with it some apparent liabilities. And I think we are saying that we can have experiential consciousness of these, and many other, gut level realities.

B: Speaking about those moments when being the oppressor is personally painful, I would say that having access to, being in touch with, and knowing intimately one's own racism and sexism can be shattering.

L: That reminds me of a personal experience. In a recent theological discussion group one of the white male participants whom I perceived as honestly trying to come to terms with contemporary realities, said: "Yes, there are problems in the western white male theological tradition, but at its high points, it has declared a universal truth." He said this eloquently and passionately. Then, in a very quiet way, one of the black men in the group spoke up: "It is very interesting how you said that—about the high points—because that isn't true. It doesn't speak any truth to me." Essentially, the black man was saying that the white man's open, sincere, almost confessional statement was in fact racist. The point was, and is, that straight white males have a way of assuming that when they speak, they speak for everyone.

B: The same oppressive style is operative with regard to women.

L: Obviously: because males depend on a series of marriage myths, women see themselves objectified through sexism. Few males, for example, feel themselves unattracted to *Playboy*; the magazine is sexist and oppressive but—let's face it—most of us like it!

B: For men, sexual objectification also includes the locating of sexuality primarily in the context of relationships with women. And it includes the expectations one places upon a wife or mother in terms of her maintenance of a smoothly running home.

L: We can also be in touch with sexism simply via our language, the use of "man" as a generic term for example. Feminine adjectives often are used derisively or as symbols of evil. Though I think *our* experiences with homosexual oppression have been less immediate, there are equally convincing examples in that area. What we are saying, generally, is that straight white males can be in touch at both an intellectual level and an emotional level—a gut level—regarding the cries of others' oppression and our own dehumanization. These are ways to come to consciousness and awareness.

B: The second phase of coming to consciousness, then, we seem to be identifying with visceral knowledge, both our own and that of others.

L: But we can't design gut level responses. If we are aware, they will happen. We will see how we oppress others, and how we in turn are thereby dehumanized. The two are so interrelated. Our straightness and whiteness and maleness provide us with pleasure at the expense of others. We gain self-confidence from work and career. But the product of our work is often the suffering of others. Things that make us feel good, give meaning to our lives, and build positive self-images indirectly oppress other people. On the surface the corporate executive, for example, is acknowledged as a great "success," but many corporations are connected with the oppressed of the world. We derive confidence from professionalism. We like individualism and competition. These are male virtues, and we feel good about them. But as these attributes are exercised, others lose. The games we play are stacked in our favor, and the socializations we go through prepare us for them. Liberation for straight white males has to do with alternatives to all this and more.

B: You mention characteristics built into who we are. It is difficult and frightening to be in touch with them at all.

L: Coming to this gut level awareness cuts us off from things we used to be able to do and enjoy. For example, feminism is making it harder for straight white males to maintain typical patterns of behavior toward women. In a sense, we are cut off from those old patterns, be they dating, traditional family roles, or public behavior in the presence of women.

B: And as one is being cut off, an original kind of innocent pleasure is undermined.

L: It's like finding out that Santa Claus doesn't really exist. Somehow that knowledge doesn't make the whole thing quite as much fun any more.

B: We have spoken about intellectual awareness and about internal feelings, but there is also a third level of our coming to consciousness: the external challenges. Here we could include the fact of liberation movements themselves, and their ramifications for us. More specifically, however, I have in mind such a thing as a straight white male being displaced in a job by a black, a woman, or a homosexual—or being shunted aside while others get the promotions.

L: Let me add something from my personal perspective. I am one who is not content with doing something insignificant; I have to have some significant work to do. As I see it, in American society, such opportunities often open up via a graduate school education. But now I must admit to myself that when I am finished with professional, graduate education, there may be few openings for me, partly because of the presence and attractiveness of blacks, women, and homosexuals competing for the same opportunities. In a sense, I feel caught. It is difficult to deal with these dilemmas.

B: Situations such as you describe reveal just how threatened we can be, and perhaps are, as straight white males today.

L: What do you see going on with senior men in college concerning the job market?

B: Unlike what we might hope would be the result of the contemporary liberation struggles and their implications for vocational opportunities, I see a strong backlash. In a sense, that proves our point about dehumanization. What I mean is that college seniors—men—are cautious, more intentional, less imaginative, less willing to take risks, and more pragmatic and job-oriented than women. Men seemed scared, vocationally uptight. They think in terms of getting requirements out of the way and getting a job. They are not asking questions about other options. For them, the American dream seems alive and well.

L: I guess this is an example of further polarization and reaction. How does the situation compare with that of a few years ago?

B: In terms of risk-taking, thinking of alternatives, and straight white male sensitivity to the issues we are discussing, I think there was more of it then than now.

L: Regarding the challenges straight white males are experiencing, they want to respond creatively, but seem immobilized. There is existential malaise. There don't seem to be as many options open as before. These challenges cut deeply into the favoritism we are accustomed to receiving. This anticipation of further challenges should force us to ask how we can prepare for the costs of change, for there will be real costs for straight white males to bear. But apparently that's not happening if your assessment is correct.

B: Of course, the oppression from which straight white males have profited has been costly for blacks, women, and gays too. So it is no surprise that a movement away from those costs will incur new and different ones. I guess liberation for us will initially come in the form of deprivation. Let's face it, if that is correct, we will not have the prominence—or comfort—we once did.

L: Crisis, challenge, and crunch are important words for us to consider. We must recognize that some of our sources of meaning are corrupt. Pleasure and innocence are on the wane. At the same time, it makes no sense to simply switch people around and put men in meaningless places. What we must seek out is an alternative style. An important question is this: How can I, as a straight white male, affirm myself and my being, and how can I find positive roots of meaning and identity after having recognized the corruptions of which we have spoken? This is a haunting question, especially for straight white males who are yet young enough to be facing career decisions. They still stand on this side of having status, power, and prestige.

B: There is a paradox here, and it's almost amusing to watch: To the extent that social policy regarding "minority" rights results from the contemporary liberation movements and is codified in social institutions, the straight white males who will be initiating, establishing, and enforcing this legislation are actually those who will not really be affected by it, since they are already in power and can't be dislodged. For example, in the university setting, tenured faculty members can support "minority" hiring, knowing full well that their jobs are secure. Those who will be affected are those moving up the ladder, or about to get on it. The practical impact of these movements will not affect the establishment so much as the potential establishment.

L: Add to these observations an international perspective. Even if the American pie could be divided equally, there would still be much oppression worldwide. In other words, even if the American establishment is affected, the negative impact will be nothing compared with Third World suffering.

B: Maybe we are suggesting that middle-range straight white males, if they are motivated at all by self-interest, should be getting in touch with the oppressed. Either they sneak under the establishment wire before a black, a woman, or a homosexual gets their job, or else they begin to understand how their welfare is linked to that of the oppressed. Perhaps their future lies with the latter option, though that may be a naïve suggestion since I doubt that the liberation movements we are talking about will have that much impact that soon.

L: The situation poses a difficult question. At one level straight white males are being cut out of the pie, and at another level they must ask how they can direct their lives in a meaningful way into work that seems significant—without buying into that same pie as presently maintained on the American scene. What kinds of work can we think about doing? What lifestyles can be created which do not depend upon oppression? These are hard questions.

B: The liberation we are talking about involves a process of uprooting. We are speaking of breaking away or renouncing certain sources of identity and meaning in our lives as demonic, corrupt, and the essence of oppressorhood. We can't quit being the oppressors, and we will always be in this situation due to benefits received. But for those who choose to move on the straight white male end of liberation, away from oppressorhood, there must be some new sources of identity and meaning and strength which sustain us. I think I'm asking how straight white males will sustain themselves in the process which, in many respects, is disadvantageous to their own well-being. We've said it is in the interest of straight white males to be concerned about liberation. But we've also admitted that in other ways this liberation is not at all in our self-interest. If we say liberation is important and necessary, then how are we supported in a quest that is disruptive, revealing, and negative for us?

HOMELESS SPIRITS

L: I don't think anyone has adequate responses to the issues you just raised, but let me think aloud about mine. As oppressors, our spirit is possessed by the structures of domination, as are the meaning and identity we derive from them. If we uproot our spirit and selves from traditional roles, if we depart from the satisfaction of achievement, if we give up competition and the benefits of affluence, we end up in a situation characterized by an emptiness of spirit. We can call it meaninglessness. There seems to be nothing we can take hold of, have faith in, and move with. There are no sure foundations for who we are. We are leaving one spiritual home and heading out on the road. But people can't stay on the road forever. It is hard to accept and live with existential meaninglessness. For if confronted with it too long, we will revert into oppressorhood—unless we find some place to move with the spirit that puts us in touch with new roots of identity and meaning. We need something to sustain us in the breaking away and renunciation connected with liberation, and eventually discover something new upon which to grasp hold.

B: What are you prepared to propose?

L: Some aspects of the Judeo-Christian tradition offer resources to which I am attracted. I mean parts of the biblical tradition, the theological tradition, and even elements in the church's historical tradition. In all of these there are examples of people who chose not to stand in the mainstream of their culture—groups of oppressors who renounced their oppressorhood. Incidentally, these traditions are also full of oppressors who renounced nothing. There aren't many examples of those who stood in resistance and renunciation. But the Confessing Church in Germany, the contemporary Catholic Left, and some religious communities come to mind. Of course, there are other examples too where people who had access to the mainstream nonetheless stood on the social margins. One can learn some theology by looking at how these and other groups understood themselves in the light of religious faith.

B: Let me put it differently, in terms of freedom. Fundamentally, I see freedom as the essence of what it means to be a human being. Human beings must be free to grow, change, and develop their human potential. Freedom is basic to legitimate order.

Perhaps such an affirmation is not common sense, but a statement of faith in what human existence was meant to be. What I conclude from it is that the circumstances, processes, and contexts which inhibit freedom are then by definition inhuman. Those who stand on the side of such forces and/or benefit from them are inhibiting freedom for others, and eventually for themselves. I think there is an interconnection between human beings in the world. To be human, in a very basic sense, is to have contact with and responsibility for others. As long as one is enslaved, all are enslaved. That's the kind of linkage I mean.

L: How does that sustain you?

B: What that means is that if one is committed to one's own humanness and that of others, one is committed to freedom. The quest for freedom is a prominent and common feature of the black, the feminist, and the homosexual revolutions. Hence, if I am to be free, I must also be committed to their freedom, and vice versa. But beyond that argument, to the extent that my own point of reference is theological, it seems to me that one of the big themes in the biblical tradition is the idea of freedom. Included in it are numerous paradigms which illustrate the human struggle for freedom amidst various forms of enslavement.

L: Let me ask again what sustains you? Are you talking about possibilities for transforming one's spirit? Are you saying we must listen to the traditions which speak about freedom and put ourselves in tune with those who have gone up this road before? It seems to me that such stories offer one a sense of not being alone in the present. The spirit of freedom lives on. And somehow it is possible to believe, via these traditions, that freedom eventually overcomes the forces that oppose freedom. Straight white males can begin to experience the profound witness of these traditions as they break away from old identities. We can feel new life, new power, and a new spirit.

B: At a personal level, what sustains me is the excitement emerging out of prospects for growth and change as I am freed up from that which has socialized me, freed up for new kinds of living.

NOTE

*Julius Lester, speech delivered at the conference on "Chaos Invading Cosmos—A Reshaping of Hope," (University of Kansas, 1973).

The Christian or messianic story documents its "saving reality and power" in a paradigmatic movement from a politics of confrontation to a politics of transfiguration whose code words are: *submission*, *silence*, and *transfiguration* itself. These code words identify the boundaries toward which and within which the dynamics of revolutionary passion, promise, and struggle are liberated from self-destruction and shaped instead for a new and divinely appointed order of human affairs in which time and space are ordered so as to make room for freedom.*

—PAUL L. LEHMANN

10. An Agenda

Glenn R. Bucher and Charles E. Lindner

SUPPORT IN GROUPS

L: A large part of liberation for straight white males, as we have said, involves a coming to consciousness, and one phase of that is assembling a story which enables us to understand who we are. There are public and private dimensions to straight white male identity. For me, the most prominent aspect of the public side is career, whereas being a family man dominates the private sector. The two sides intersect, of course. Coming to consciousness should put one in touch with career and family issues. Even though it's difficult to get hold of the working out of consciousness, it must manifest itself in praxis. I think a basic model for getting to the practical aspects of liberation is an engagement-reflection model. One must be involved in liberation pursuits, and then reflect upon what he is doing. Then we go back to action, and come to reflection again—a critical, and dynamic process.

B: I think telling a story is one way to provide groundwork on which to build an agenda. Out of it should emerge things to do as one sees the intersections of his story with that of others. Liber-

134

ation is a matter not only of thinking, but also of acting, as you have said. If one is involved in engagement-reflection, then this should provide movement forward as one becomes clearer about what one needs to move away from, and toward.

L: Yes, the assembling and the telling of the story bring to acute consciousness the limitations and problems, and the places where one needs to change. But change is difficult because straight white males are in an ambiguous position. They experience criticism on the one hand and immobilization on the other. They are being told to choose which side they are on. There are choices, but it is hard to decide where and when to change. So I think the issue of liberation must be brought back into the area of lifestyle, but remain connected to the larger structural context as well.

B: I agree that activity leading to liberation is not always clear in terms of when, where, and how to move. To be sure, it will not be glamorous. It probably will not eventuate in public acts. Liberation activity will likely begin at the level of *not* doing, rather than trying to do something new. By *not* doing, straight white males will in fact be doing a new thing. That brings to mind again the notion of renunciation; no matter how confused one is, at least he can push and nudge where he is simply by way of giving up some things.

L: The way you emphasize the difficulty of action suggests to me that straight white males need support systems for what they do.

B: I think we can begin to put together an agenda for ourselves, based on what we are involved in and related to. But we definitely need help in doing this.

L: What to do at the social and political level, or in terms of specific political tactics, is difficult to determine.

B: I sense throughout our discussions that we both want to resist a basically liberal model vis-à-vis social change.

L: I agree. Liberals, acting more as individuals than as a corporate presence, have only dealt with public issues and not with lifestyles. The reaction against that is to examine and work exclusively on styles of life. But let's admit that this can also be one-sided and, in fact, more dangerous, because it can lead to withdrawal, to the search for a pure position. If one withdraws and insists that he is not benefiting from oppression, then he must be reminded that meanwhile the structures of domination roll on full speed. If one is serious about liberation, one must deal with structures and systems. That will be difficult without a liberating context which provides support. I think the kind of positive movement of which we speak arises from within support communities where the commitment is to freedom. Here one can find the encouragement to examine and work on the social and personal dimensions of life through individual and systemic change.

B: Are you talking about straight white male support communities or consciousness-raising groups?

L: The consciousness-raising group I am afraid is largely ineffectual. Basically it brings together persons who are living a traditional, mainline lifestyle, yet starting to reflect and think about issues. The consciousness-raising group is, for them, a secondary situation, not their primary home.

B: But most straight white males are not even minimally involved in consciousness-raising, and here we sit talking about some dramatic changes in behavior that can come about only through support communities. In fact, it is not exaggerated to say that most straight white males haven't yet even listened intently to what blacks, women, and homosexuals have long been saying!

L: That's a good check. But watch out! I don't think there is that much distance between those who haven't yet heard the "minorities," those doing consciousness-raising, and those described as our ideal straight white males. The basic question is how much we share a commitment to freedom and to change. That's the issue. Let's not criticize even an initial awareness. Remember, it's hard to change quickly. But let me get back to our notion of a corporate context. At initial levels of awareness, consciousness-raising groups can be good and effective. Of course, they can also be introverted; such groups obviously have limits—but at least they are corporate!

B: In one sense, there is something suspicious about a group of men coming together to raise their consciousness. Probably some of these groups (and there aren't that many!) arose because people wanted to share their hurts. The disruption of the times brings people together. In a sense, they have come to tell their stories. And as a result, their awareness might be increased. If consciousness-raising leads to new intentional behavior supported by the group, then that is good. If anything is clear it is that straight white males need support wherever they can find it.

L: A male support group, which implies a sharing situation, will itself be difficult for people like us to handle, because we are such private people. Our hurts are private. That speaks to a form of dehumanization. I can understand how a conscious-ness-raising group might be perceived as intimidating, but it is a necessary risk we must take. After all, the first big leap forward might come about as a result of having shared some hurts.

B: It occurs to me that built into the American straight white male culture are many groups which could be transformed into consciousness-raising groups. I'm thinking of "service" clubs (Kiwanis, Lions, Rotary), country clubs, drinking clubs, card clubs, even men's Sunday school classes.

L: These groups are support groups all right! But as you well know, they support what we think needs to be broken down, namely, traditional straight white male images and models. These clubs certainly serve a purpose. I guess in terms of our talk, they enable the oppressor to continue on his merry way.

B: Obviously, I agree. My point was that support groups are not foreign to the experience of straight white males. In fact, they are integral to it. That's how we got to be the way we are. I don't have much hope for the clubs I mentioned changing direc-tion. New ones will need to be formed. But at least support is not foreign to our lives if we think about it a moment.

L: One other thought: the support we are talking about in-volves a great deal of vulnerability and openness. And that is foreign to our experience. As we ourselves have discovered in these discussions, it is hard to open up.

B: I agree. I wonder how typical we are, both in terms of our difficulty with discussion and regarding what we are about. One can look around and observe some straight white males who are already into what seem to be important forms of alternative be-havior. But one gets the sense sometimes that faddism is about to set in. I guess one must accept the legitimacy of what appear to be superficial alternatives, and hope they don't become fads. If we are correct about the need for straight white males to re-nounce, then let's be clear: renunciation is hard work, not fun.

L: There will be faddish things developing as straight white males try to break away from oppressorhood, but these may not reflect freedom. Fads are easy answers. Small token gestures which acknowledge the need for change are good, but they don't indicate a radical break. I think liberation for straight white males must be thought of now in terms of renunciation. And to reiterate, I believe the context for legitimate renunciation is a group of straight white males honestly sharing hurts and support-

ing changes. Let's not forget that we have spoken of personal
and systemic changes. A decision to make lifestyle the root of
change cannot be a decision to make it the whole of change.

B: Lifestyle is simply the place where renunciation can begin
to happen.

L: Yes, that can be the beginning but it is not easy to pre-
scribe specifically the rest of the agenda for renunciation. We
certainly cannot do that here, except for ourselves. I think spe-
cifics can only emerge out of a common support group which
comes together to face issues and create actions.

B: You are saying to me that in the final analysis, each
straight white male has control over one thing—himself. Yes, we
must be concerned about public policy. But more important—
because more implementable—is each straight white male thinking about his own behavior and interactions. One can at least
begin at the individual level with something creative.

L: One of the reasons we need to be involved in corporate
settings is because individuals have a hard time thinking alone
about systemic matters. A group situation tends to connect the
individual with other individuals and with structural and systemic
issues. Here is where straight white males can get the whole
picture.

RENUNCIATION

B: We have suggested that the first creative action of straight
white males must take the form of individuals saying no to things
that ordinarily come our way. The idea has a lot of moral clout
attached to it. We are implying that people must make a willful,
intentional decision to give up some of what they have.
We seem convinced that it can be done. In other words, we are
asking people to affect adversely their own self-interest and do
something that is not particularly rational, something that ordinarily they wouldn't do. We are linking straight white male liberation to exceptional behavior. If we really think we can do that,
then we are saying that straight white males can voluntarily give
up some of their power. Both of us have learned enough from the
"realists" to know that power usually responds only when
threatened, that it doesn't give up on itself except when forced.
Certainly blacks, women, and homosexuals will bear that out.
They're not coming to straight white males and asking—or
waiting—for us to respond out of our magnanimous hearts. They
are demanding and taking. Are we somehow assuming that on
the one hand, straight white males are more demonic than most,

and on the other, that they are also capable of sensitive, moral behavior?

L: You seem to be equating renunciation with goodwill and suggesting that straight white male piety will lead to proper action. That's not renunciation as I understand it.

B: Renunciation for me implies giving up what has been mine.

L: I agree. But straight white males are not in an unambiguous position when it comes to renunciation. Renunciation doesn't arise out of consciousness-raising. It takes place at a home you've left already in spirit, but one you are still attached to. It's like a final break with an old romance—one you've basically known isn't going to make it. But it still hurts to break it up. I don't associate renunciation with the response: "My goodness, I'm evil; my piety has been appealed to; and because I have so much goodwill, I will act morally." Yes, renunciation is a willful decision. But I see another dimension to it in terms of a person being transformed who responds because of his own commitment to freedom. In other words, freedom takes primacy over oppressorhood. There is conflict and struggle. The old roots are there, but renunciation is initiated out of one's own quest for a freer self.

B: Renunciation then is saying no to external structures and selves, the vitality of which is already gone?

L: Yes, but where the vitality lingers on, and our security in it.

B: Let me apply that notion to the example of the nuclear family. Some people involved in that institution have come to see it as somewhat limiting. By that I mean they are tired of the individualism, consumerism, privatism, and sexism which dominate it. Now we're saying that part of the process of liberation involves coming to an awareness of that narrowness. That's followed by straight white males renouncing some of the luxuries of that situation, in terms of the time and space it provides them to do what they need and want. What I'm puzzled about is that renunciation in this situation is already based on a well-developed awareness. What about the straight white male who doesn't share that view? Are you saying that before anything can be changed, one must know the corruptibility of the present structures?

L: You seem to want to say that guilt will help us change. Let's face it, I don't think many straight white males will change *period*, no matter what the motive. We are speaking here to those who already have a critical sense, and perhaps raising questions for those who don't. I do think we must see the demonic in the existence we presently live before we can be motivated to change. But guilt won't do it. If you are still deriving pleasure and meaning from a situation, and know only that someone else is telling you that what you're doing doesn't make sense and is oppressing them, you are not going to do anything about it. You might take a look, but that's all. I think what motivates people into authentic change is that when they see oppression but feel good about that to which they are attached, they will still seek out freedom, pull themselves away, and risk saying no. Critical sensitivity motivates them to consider a meaningful step forward toward some alternative. In other words, their own humanity lies in the balance, even though part of it is still caught up in the spirit of death. I just don't think people will change simply because they feel guilty.

B: I suspect the awareness of which we speak might be facilitated by blacks, women, and homosexuals clamoring even louder for freedom amidst oppressive structures. What we are hoping is that straight white males will see what these other groups are talking about, and discover how limited those structures are in which they themselves live.

L: Conflicts will exist within ourselves: at one and the same time we will want to leave the old structures and we will appreciate how vital they are for us. In other words, we will have a conflict accepting conflict. One must come to awareness of the fact that though what I'm doing means a lot to me, it is perceived differently by others.

B: Some of the liberated behavior we undertake will be inspired no doubt by increased sensitivity, while some will be forced upon us by blacks, women, and homosexuals. In other words, some will be motivated by true awareness and others by guilt. Sometimes action will precede consciousness; other times the opposite will be the case. Here is the dynamic between action and reflection, reflection and action. I think it's a realistic assessment of what can happen.

L: I don't like the idea of renunciation not being a free act. I don't mean free of pain; there will always be risk, hurt, and anxiety. But action must be taken. One does it because one believes in self. The person who is motivated purely by guilt is not a free person. For example, I don't think men should be defined by the feminist movement. If men are pushed around by it and immediately agree to "demands" before they believe in what is being proposed, then acting will not be an affirmation, but a negation. To say: "I don't believe this but since one of the oppressed says it is legitimate, I will respond," is to be motivated by very suspicious factors with which I have real problems.

B: I think people can engage in actions to which they are not intellectually and emotionally committed, hoping that an understanding of those actions will follow them. Perhaps, it could be argued, the actions themselves will reveal something not previously apparent.

L: I agree to an extent, but I'm still suspicious. What you are saying can lead to fads. I don't find deep intentions toward liberation rooted in what you are saying. If straight white males respond in fickle ways, their intentionality is gone. No reflection on the action is taking place. And here is the potential for reaction. One might well end up saying; "I lost my personhood to those movements." My response is: "No, you lost your 'self' in not making decisions for freedom." I don't trust liberation efforts which do not affirm persons and their individuality. Some males that I know personally have been devastated by the women's movement because they failed to do anything other than respond automatically to what was demanded. What one ends up with is a "non-self" which does no one any good.

B: Probably we are not talking about an exclusive set of motivational factors, but a complex assortment.

L: I guess so. Related to this, let me say something else about consciousness-raising groups and renunciation. My suspicion is that some straight white males may want to stay in such groups forever, talking about their hurts until they are comfortable with the changes they want to make. The problem is that change may never come about due to the comforts. In other words, they will have been "stroked" to death. People get into the trap of saying; "I'm OK being normal until I work my problems out because I'm overwhelmed with all these difficulties and changes." That is wallowing in one's problems. Consciousness-raising as I understand it must create the foundation for change. It should not be indulgent but lay out some ground rules.

ALTERNATIVE SOURCES OF STRENGTH

B: Since we are talking about an agenda for straight white males, admittedly in an inevitably general way, let me ask where all this talk of liberation is headed. Aren't those who emphasize freedom and want liberation in danger of precipitating a social and personal situation that is eventually anarchistic? I can imagine diffuse and conflicting results that could be perceived as far worse than what we now have. I guess I'm asking about guidelines and criteria for evaluating authentic liberation, as well as new forms of oppression. Is our talk going anywhere, or are we simply revolving in a vicious circle?

L: I had the same thought. Is what we are doing futile? Are we merely rebelling against the way things are? Maybe we should just face the fact that in the world as we know it, some will have a better lot than others, and nothing can be changed much.

B: And to go on, how shall one evaluate the legitimacy and/or illegitimacy of the liberation struggles themselves? How do we know we are taking one step forward and not two steps backwards? Are there any guidelines and definitions? When we talk about wholeness and humanness, what do these words mean?

L: We are coming to ever increased awareness of the costs, oppressions, and dehumanizations of the present. All we can do is be informed by our own agendas, the traditions and stories which point to a more human life, and try to move in a new direction. There are no absolute formulas. When we speak of liberation we are talking about a dynamic life, a dialectic, and changes and shifts. We can only move toward a goal which human beings, on their own, will not be fully able to achieve.

B: To go back to my point, the liberation struggles of the present are terribly disruptive in all sorts of ways. Many people, the oppressed and the oppressors, feel that. It would be so easy to stick with the status quo.

L: What you mean is that these struggles are terribly disruptive for the *oppressors*. Some say, for example, that the Civil Rights movement led to violence. That's nonsense! It was the negative reactions to that movement that produced violence. The question is: who's being disrupted by whom and for what reasons? What is normal for some is not normal for others. The *normal* is what is disruptive. You are asking whether any change can be accomplished. What can we do except trust in the possibilities, and believe that life is dynamic and not static.

B: I have two responses. First, I don't agree that liberation struggles are disruptive only for the oppressor. Some of those conditioned as the oppressed have had their lives upset by talk of liberation. Probably we would say this is a legitimate kind of disruption. But it is that! And secondly, in terms of how one responds to the ambiguity of change, in the end there is only one thing I can affirm. That is the potentiality of human life, its possibilities, and its latent and real goodness. In the turmoil of struggle it often seems that everything is blown apart. I have in mind one's world view, one's roles, one's sense of right and wrong. Nothing much is left unturned by the liberation struggles. And so one has to decide what it is he can hold onto.

L: Now the issue is clearer. We are asking about one's security. That's a crucial question for straight white males. The places in which we now find security are caught in the winds of change.

B: Maybe that forces us to talk about areas in which renunciation can take place in hopes that different types of strength emerge. I assume that would include dismantling the power and support that have been privileged sources for straight white males. I guess one exchanges them for the spirit of freedom. Presumably we believe that new sources of identity and meaning can emerge from freedom.

L: Let me say something about the notion of career in this regard, since traditionally that certainly has been a source of one kind of strength. As a young straight white male, I must face the fact that I need to be engaged in some significant work. Traditionally, that has been defined for me by degrees, profession, and established career. Now the problems here are multiple. If one goes this traditional route, one is forced to buy into what is middle-class. And along with that come lifestyle, power, and affluence. Of course, one usually ends up working for some institution. Some of these are the institutions that oppress people. In essence, one's career can easily become the center of one's identity. That's why raising this question is so threatening.

B: What are your thoughts about alternative work and how that is related to the security we mentioned?

L: Words like authority, power, control, and dominance come to mind. Males traditionally define power as power over people. They want to control situations. Males will have a hard time taking orders. And so the question about work is this: Is there work in which I can be engaged which does not require control of situations and dependence upon others? We need to discover careers that offer flexibility, so that other aspects of our lifestyle can be developed. We need work that gives us time to be engaged in politics, in group living, and so on. We must find work that does not impose a whole network of menial jobs on others.

B: I agree. I struggle with that in my role as professor. Attached to it are attributes such as authority, power, control, and dominance, at least as the role is usually defined. As a result, people expect us to function along those lines and, in fact, sometimes are immobilized when we don't. My question is this: If I take renunciation and liberation seriously, can I still be a professor? If the answer is yes, what must I then do to transform the way I function? In other words, how does one get out of the authority and power bag? I think it is possible to transform that role. Rethinking how one perceives and relates to "students" is a good place to start. The transformation, however, will also need to cut more deeply into lifestyle, the manner in which one perceives one's skills, one's limitations, and one's way of inquiring about the truth. I guess a related question I have has to do with those who presently find themselves in other vocations. For example, what options does the Junior Executive in General Motors presently have? He doesn't have as fluid a situation as the professor. Does he have alternatives short of changing vocations if he is fully committed to straight white male liberation? And if he must get out to exercise his liberation, what are the implications for the American economy as the straight white male is related to it?

L: The only middle option I see is staying where one is and raising the moral issues. Maybe General Motors could become a manufacturer of mass transit, but of course it won't. Actually, I don't have much hope regarding this matter of career options. But we must begin to rethink the ways important work is done and the presuppositions of it. We must ask how much roles can be transformed. The Maoist would say that no people can spend all their time in elite kinds of work. All must be involved in producing material goods necessary for the society. No one can have an inordinate amount of power and privilege. Menial tasks must be shared. Across the board, people must be freed up to be creative. This is where I see the matter of liberation going as it relates to careers.

B: You are really alluding to alternative forms of living which try to move beyond responsibility, success, and social power in the typical sense. Others I might add are economic cooperatives which rely on such methods as communal salary pools, short work assignments for some, and shared child rearing.

L: Something I often think about is what kinds of compromise positions there are, and how far one can compromise. To insist on the radical alternatives is to cut out compromises that might be legitimate. Obviously the American economic system doesn't allow for all men to consider leaving their jobs. But the realistic options are scarce.

B: What we are saying, though, is that renunciation means saying no to traditional vocational and career options because they implicate others in oppression. And furthermore, straight white males need to be freed from them for their own good. No doubt the cynic will remind us that if straight white males renounce their options, then blacks, women, and gays will move in to take their places. And that may not be much of an advance, given the fact that the same structures, assumptions, and goals will no doubt be operative. Let's be clear about it, those "minorities" may or may not bring a different world view from that of the males they replace.

L: Again, what can we say now except that straight white males have to be about the business that is obviously theirs. When that is completed, we can worry about what has happened to blacks, women, and homosexuals on their way to the establishment. I think our point here is that for straight white males, the career has functioned as a great support system for what we are about. So one is forced to conclude that if liberation is to be authentic, the career syndrome will have to be challenged, along with the sources of strength that attend it.

THE FUTURE

B: There is despair and hope in our comments on liberation and where it will lead. We've admitted that, in one sense, we don't know where it's going. The future seems rather unsure. And we've suggested that straight white males won't have full control over the total consequences of liberation. Though we may be able to act creatively on our own, we just don't know how that will fit into the dynamics being let loose by the liberation struggles of blacks, women, homosexuals, and the Third World.

This kind of ambiguity is not easy for us to accept. We seem to need to be in control of events. We want to be rational, intentional, and purposeful about them, knowing that the way history works itself out is within our power to manipulate. What we are saying is that this will not be possible, even if it were desirable. To be sure, all this is rather disarming. I guess we must just accept the fact that we don't have all the answers, which suggests that straight white males must entrust the future to others, and follow their vision.

L: Another compulsion I think we are under is to insure

straight white males that the results of liberation won't be as threatening as they seem. But they will be. One need only think of the career implications we have mentioned to underline that point. The challenges are clearly revolutionary, though I use that word with hesitation. I don't know how prepared straight white males are to meet these challenges.

B: Is that to be the ending note in our discussion? To conclude by saying that the consequences of liberation are clearly revolutionary, for ourselves as well as others, and that we don't know the rest is to leave the future and ourselves very much in the air.

L: Perhaps the future is not quite that unclear. We are still very much a part of the mainstream. How we will cut ourselves off from it, stand outside it, and still maintain contact and dialogue with it are real issues. Maybe I'm saying I'm still committed to the status quo, or want to be. Or perhaps I want to insist that if changes come, they must come in Middle America, because that's where the problems are. This is very tough to sort out. In a sense, we are saying that we don't want too many compromises, but we also want to be in touch where things must be changed. Keeping one's head in the right place is hard. Compromise can be very seductive. And seductive compromise creates a continuous circle of seduction. One must decide where one wants to be.

B: It sounds like you're saying one can choose to compromise or not. Do you mean that? In a sense, we must begin with the affirmation that we are already compromised. There is no way we can get out of that, even if it were possible. We can only work at the compromises we have made and want to make. We must admit that the affluence we already enjoy enables us to sit down, talk, and write books. People who don't know where the next day's food is coming from can't do that.

L: I guess it's a question of deciding which compromises one can live with. At some point, perhaps some compromises will be rejected. But in making that decision, one is haunted by the communication break-off. Of course, these are not only the dilemmas of straight white males. Blacks, women, and homosexuals face the same issues.

B: Are we saying that the place to do renunciation and work on liberation is in the middle of Middle America? That is the suburb, where I am and you were. We agreed there are clear limits to living in such situations.

L: The suburb is seductive. It forces one to believe in normalcy. Then to break from that is difficult. If the break comes, you'll be accused of cutting yourself off. But there is a real question about who cut off whom. Some view alternate living as deviant and irrelevant. But in a sense, those who live in Middle America are deviant. They are cut off because they are so out of touch with the realities of the world.

B: But I can cut myself off too. Some go to the farm, others to the city. In one respect, these moves represent a removing of oneself. There's some irony here in that we are also insisting that straight white males working on liberation must remain in touch with the homes they have left, while at the same time saying no.

L: In the city one can be either in touch with the oppressed or oblivious to them. That option of contact with those who hurt is not as alive in suburban America. That can't be disregarded. Sometimes I think that the suburb presents an almost hopeless and futile situation. Maybe that's symptomatic. Actually, I think things are quite hopeless generally in terms of any meaningful, structural change in our time. There aren't many signs of hope amidst realities such as population growth, food shortages, terrorism, and nuclear war. Things no doubt will get much worse. That conclusion raises the question about how one is to live in these times and without responding in reactionary ways.

B: Hopelessness is hard for straight white males to understand. We need to think something can be done about a situation and that we can do it. But, you're right, hopelessness seems abundant. I guess in the final analysis I'm forced to draw again on theological resources. What I understand the biblical story to be about, in addition to what I've already said, is that amidst hopelessness which seems permanent there will always be surprises of joy and peace and renewal. Somehow when it is all said and done, hope emerges again to be actualized and lived out.

L: I have a couple responses. One is to ask how much worse things must get? You speak of hope, and I like to believe in it. But when does that hope become one more form of hope which refuses to face despair? I both believe and don't believe in hope. My other response is that I think you're right about the theological resources. The voices of oppression are signs of hope. Biblical faith says that when change comes about, these people are harbingers of that change. This leaves me, as a straight white male, in an ambiguous position, because those movements are not available to me. I guess that means we must get out of the way, and let hope blossom.

B: The tasks for straight white males are twofold, as I see it.

We must stay out of, and we must get into, the way. If we take seriously forms of renunciation, we may at strange places and times find ourselves beside those who are struggling for liberation. I think a form of identification and camaraderie can happen. If we renounce enough things in enough areas at enough times, we may end up in the same place as the oppressed. That won't happen quickly, but it could happen. And secondly, the biblical story says that expressions of hope happen amidst despair, and come as gifts, as unexpected occurrences, to those who stand and wait in the right place. Hope is not fully or finally a human creation.

L: I think the prospects for hope in history will diminish, not increase. In fact, the possibility for an explicit human tragedy is quite good. Ten thousand human beings are dying every week from starvation. That is a hard fact which we know hardly anything about. It isn't exactly the same as complaining about high food prices. And the situation with regard to population and food can only get worse. I think the hope is very slim that the human community can avert a massive tragedy. Within these circumstances, how can straight white males keep from being more reactionary? How can the voices of the oppressed be kept alive? To talk of straight white male liberation in this context is, in a real sense, to hope against hopelessness.

B: My concluding thought is that the most essential statement anyone can make about another human being is that he/she is indeed that—a human being. Persons are unique. When everything else is stripped away, we have one essential connection with others—our corporate humanity. In the final analysis, it is the only factor that matters. Hence, there ought to be no question about the highest priority for the human community. The only thing that matters is human life and its essential necessities. Most of the rest of the world—including many blacks, women, and homosexuals—don't have those necessities, necessities which of course go beyond mere physical survival to include dignity, respect, and other psychosocial needs. Most straight white males do. And many of us can decide how those necessities will be distributed, or guaranteed, or nurtured. The implications of that fact for straight white male liberation will keep us busy a long time!

NOTE

*Paul L. Lehmann, *The Transfiguration of Politics* (New York: Harper & Row, 1975), pp. 246–47.